Che [illegible] ategy

Chess and Corporate Strategy is an intriguing journey through cognitive psychology, artificial intelligence, and game theory. The innovative methodology employed by the author leverages the metaphor of chess to furnish a compendium of corporate strategy, including strategic thinking, decision-making, negotiations, and leadership.

This book provides the reader with the insights and strategies of chess champions, without the need for years of study and practice. Throughout this book, captivating episodes from the rich history of the game of chess weave seamlessly, elevating the reading experience beyond that of a conventional management publication. Every chapter is enriched by insightful interviews featuring Anatoly Karpov, the 12th chess world champion. Karpov adeptly illustrates the practical application of theoretical concepts in the professional realm through real-life examples.

This book will be a valuable resource to leaders and executives interested in innovative ways of thinking about corporate strategy and the running of a business.

Luca Desiata is an Adjunct Faculty Member at Luiss Business School, Italy.

Chess and Corporate Strategy

Luca Desiata, in collaboration with Anatoly Karpov

Routledge
Taylor & Francis Group
LONDON AND NEW YORK

Designed cover image: Yudram_TA / iStock / Getty Images Plus

First published 2025
by Routledge
4 Park Square, Milton Park, Abingdon, Oxon OX14 4RN

and by Routledge
605 Third Avenue, New York, NY 10158

Routledge is an imprint of the Taylor & Francis Group, an informa business

British Library Cataloguing-in-Publication Data
A catalogue record for this book is available from the British Library

Library of Congress Cataloging-in-Publication Data
Names: Desiata, Luca, author.
Title: Chess and corporate strategy / Luca Desiata.
Description: Abingdon, Oxon ; New York, NY : Routledge, 2025. |
Includes bibliographical references and index.
Identifiers: LCCN 2024058607 (print) | LCCN 2024058608 (ebook) |
ISBN 9781032876450 (hardback) | ISBN 9781032876443 (paperback) |
ISBN 9781003533719 (ebook)
Subjects: LCSH: Strategic planning. | Game theory. | Chess.
Classification: LCC HD30.28 .D47195 2025 (print) | LCC HD30.28
(ebook) | DDC 658.4/012—dc23/eng/20250220
LC record available at https://lccn.loc.gov/2024058607
LC ebook record available at https://lccn.loc.gov/2024058608

ISBN: 9781032876450 (hbk)
ISBN: 9781032876443 (pbk)
ISBN: 9781003533719 (ebk)

DOI: 10.4324/9781003533719

Typeset in Optima
by codeMantra

This book would not have been possible without the valuable insights contributed by the following experts, to whom I extend my deepest gratitude:

- Chess champions: Anatoly Karpov, Bachar Kouatly, Lexy Ortega.
- Corporate Managers: Rocco Sabelli, Francesco Starace, Marco Arcelli, Andrea Stolfa, Leonardo Caputo, Cristina Monacelli, Filippo Pipitone, Jean-Marc Pailhol.
- Business School Professors: Paolo Boccardelli, Luca Pirolo, Markus Venzin.
- Additional contributors: Adele Ucci, Marie Oneissi, Youssef Iraqui.

Contents

About the Author

Luca Desiata is an Adjunct Faculty Member at Luiss Business School, Italy. He is an engineer with an MBA from INSEAD. He was the CEO of the Italian State-owned company Sogin between 2016 and 2019 and the Country Manager of Enel in France and Belgium between 2013 and 2016. Previously he had worked in consulting (Accenture and Bain) and IFC (International Finance Corporation/World Bank Group) in the Balkans.

Anatoly Karpov is the 12th chess world champion

Figures

Chapter 1

Introduction

As a corporate executive, you recognize that playing chess could significantly enhance your strategic decision-making skills. Yet, the perceived time and effort needed to achieve proficiency in the game might be holding you back. Look no further! This book provides you with the insights and strategies of chess champions, without the need for years of study and practice.

So you might be wondering: What makes chess such a compelling analogy for corporate strategy? Let's explore some of its key features.

Chess to impress

Chess is referred to as the royal game due to its historical associations with royalty and aristocracy. It is traditionally linked with passion, elegance, superior intelligence and foresight, perseverance, and courage.

The game of chess has been around for millennia. Shrouded in myth and legend, its origins continue to intrigue and baffle historians. Its profound beauty and complexity have captivated mathematicians and philosophers for centuries, providing sophisticated intellectual pleasure. In recent times, chess has become a fertile ground for advancements in artificial intelligence (AI), neural networks, and decision-making algorithms. Historically, Napoleon used chess to test his military strategies, while Jacopo da Cessole drew inspiration from the game for his influential book on morality, the second most-sold book in the Middle Ages after the Bible. Even Saint Teresa of Avila, a 16th-century intellectual nun, employed chess as a metaphor to explore the dynamics of contemplation and prayer in her spiritual work "The Way of Perfection". More recently, chess has been incorporated into US military training for Marines to foster a more strategic and analytical thinking environment.

Throughout its millennia-long history, chess has consistently mirrored the spirit of its time, revealing the following fascinating geopolitical correlation.

DOI: 10.4324/9781003533719-1

During the Renaissance, when Rome and Florence dominated global culture and commerce, the world's strongest players were Italian. In the 18th and mid-19th centuries, during the Napoleonic era, this supremacy shifted to the French. Then the British, Germans, and Americans, with few exceptions. In 1972, at the height of the Cold War, the titanic clash between the Russian champion Boris Spassky and the American challenger Bobby Fischer captivated the public's attention globally and became a metaphor for the Cold War itself. In 2012, in the wake of the emergence of the Asian economic powers, the male chess world champion was Indian and the female world champion was Chinese. These cannot be mere coincidences: it appears that when a nation ascends to great power status, a portion of its assertive ethos permeates the realm of chess, often yielding world champions, thus providing the ground for this fascinating historical and geopolitical correlation.

When discussing chess in relation to Management, it is relevant to note that, throughout the 20th century, the primary advancements in AI focused on defeating human chess champions. This challenge began with Alan Turing's creation of the first algorithm to play chess, Turochamp, in 1948, and culminated in 1997 when IBM's Deep Blue software defeated the reigning world champion, Garry Kasparov, prompting experts to proclaim the end of human intelligence. However, this defeat was merely the tip of the iceberg of a broader trend that, since the mid-1990s, has seen intelligence steadily flow from human brains to computer circuits, as is illustrated in Figure 1.1, where the surge of AI strength (conventionally measured by its chess ELO rating) is plotted against the decline of human intelligence (measured by standard IQ scores).

In the corporate realm, chess has also significantly contributed to decision-making theory and cognitive psychology. Few are aware that

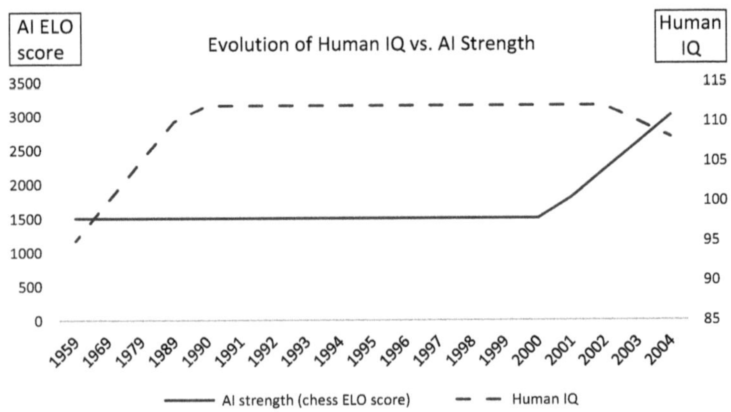

Figure 1.1 Evolution of human IQ and AI strength "AI ELO score" and "Human IQ".

the origins of strategic thinking theory trace back to the experiments conducted by Dutch psychologist and chess player Adriaan De Groot in the mid-20th century. De Groot presented chess positions to the champions of his time (1940s–1960s), prompting them to verbally articulate their mental processes for making moves. Through structured protocols and comparative analysis of these verbal reports, De Groot identified key categories of strategic thinking in chess that bear a remarkable resemblance to corporate strategic thinking.[1]

Finally, recognizing that negotiation theory is a subset of game theory, the game of chess—with its distinct characteristics of being zero-sum, asymmetrical, and featuring perfect information—can be used as a model for certain types of negotiations. For instance, the term "first mover's advantage" in negotiation terminology is a straightforward chess analogy. Furthermore, chess software has proven that the optimal strategy to win in a zero-sum sequential negotiation is the Minimax strategy, aimed at minimizing the opponent's maximum advantage by limiting their best options—a significant departure from the more instinctive negotiation strategy of bolstering one's own strengths.

Given all the evidence above, one must wonder why the parallel with corporate strategy has remained unexplored in scientific research.

More about strategy

One possible answer to why the parallel with corporate strategy has remained unexplored in scientific research is that, much like chess, the concept of strategy has been misapplied for various purposes throughout the centuries. Currently, there exists no universally accepted definition of corporate strategy. Therefore, prior to drawing parallels with chess, it is imperative that we establish a clear understanding of the concept of strategy.

The word "strategy" originated in military spheres. Etymologically it comes from the Greek στρατός ἀγός stratos agos, i.e. "he who leads (agos) the army (stratos)", meaning the science or art of the generals. Strategy is therefore the branch of military art that studies the principles of warlike operations, with the aim to define and coordinate the general plan of the war. Strategy is also known as the "Theory of the action of success in the presence of an aware opposition".

Based on these definitions involving objectives and plans, it shouldn't be hard to draw a parallel between military and corporate strategy. Finally, being chess a metaphor for military warfare, once the connection is established between military and corporate strategy, then the parallel between chess and corporate strategy naturally follows.

However, we prefer to go beyond the specificities of the military and business domains and instead define strategy in terms of broader and more abstract cognitive categories.

Therefore, the definition of strategy for our purposes is the following:

Box 1.1 Definition of strategy for chess and corporate strategy

Strategy is any scheme produced by the human mind with the aim of modifying reality.

In its simplicity, this definition will be the starting point for a systematic analysis of the "schemes" or "shortcuts" implemented by the human mind to tackle the complexity of reality.

We can expand this definition and translate it into a process for strategic thinking. This process serves as the foundation for contextualizing De Groot's discoveries from his experiments on chess champions' minds.[2]

In this process as per Figure 1.2, we can highlight two parallel layers of action. The lower part happens in the real world, and the upper part unfolds in our minds. Let's get a closer look at the different stages. The first step is conceptualization, i.e. the human mind elaborates a scheme of the current situation in the real world. During the initial phases of addressing a problem, our minds would be overwhelmed if they couldn't start organizing the multitude of external stimuli into schemes, which gradually become more detailed and intricate. Mental representations, which are communicable and shareable, can only be developed by the human mind through the utilization of conceptual categories and logical relationships.

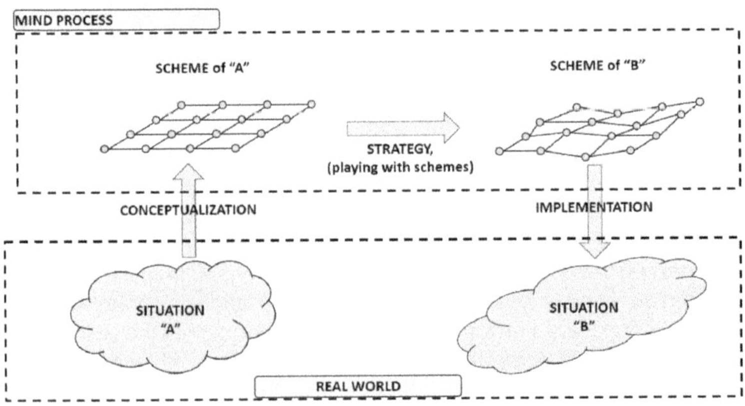

Figure 1.2 Strategic thinking process

In the following stage, our minds manipulate the scheme of reality until the initial problem is addressed and resolved. The result of this stage is a logical scheme free from the initial problem. Ultimately, this problem-free scheme is implemented into reality through an action plan. Based on this process, it follows that strategy means playing with the logical schemes of the real world.

As the strategic thinking process is "pure logic into action", then the primary quality demanded of a strategy is the inherent coherence of its components. This clarifies why, during a company's strategic plan presentation, even the slightest discrepancy between identical data presented in two different sections raises concerns about the entire approach of the proposed strategy. A minor logical inconsistency within an inherently coherent system has the potential to dismantle even the most robust strategic framework.

Finally, no framework about strategy would be complete without mentioning tactics. In the words of former chess Grandmaster Savielly Tartakower (1887–1956): "Tactics is knowing what to do when there is something to do, strategy is knowing what to do when there is nothing to do".

In our approach, we distinguish tactics from strategy depending on the available time to plan for the reaction. This time is a function of (1) the speed of evolution of reality and (2) thought processing speed. We are in the realm of strategy when our reaction times are faster than the speed of change of reality, i.e. when we have time to sit down at a table and reflect on the next course of action.

Conversely, when the reality changes faster than our reaction times, we will talk about tactics. In these situations, "reproductive" mechanisms come into play, involving immediate and instinctive responses primarily based on experience. These "tactical" reactions are essential to manage scenarios where there is no time to think or develop a plan to apply to reality.

In summary, tactics are considered as immediate reactions to events.

In chess, we talk about tactics when we can reach a material advantage through a limited number of moves, not necessarily foreseen within the overall strategy.

Similarly, in the corporate world, we talk about tactics during the implementation phase when we can achieve a target through a limited number of actions, not necessarily foreseen within the overall strategy.

Conceptual map of the parallel between chess and corporate strategy

Building upon the aforementioned framework and definitions, this book will illustrate how chess can teach valuable lessons to managers aiming

Figure 1.3 Conceptual map of the parallel between chess and corporate strategy

for success. This book is organized into two main macro-areas: strategy formulation and strategy execution, each with the following sub-chapters:

Strategy formulation:

- Cognitive psychology and strategic thinking: This section focuses on De Groot's experiments on the minds of chess champions in the 20th century[3];
- Decision-making theory: It explores the contributions of chess to the advancement of AI and decision-making methodologies.

Strategy execution:

- Strategic planning and resource allocation: This chapter will explore the military nature of business;
- Risk management: This chapter examines the ability to foresee and manage unexpected situations, even in the deterministic scenarios of a chessboard;
- Negotiation theory: This section, based on game theory, shows how the game of chess can illustrate various dynamics of zero-sum negotiations.

Finally, within this framework, leadership represents the key ingredient that binds strategy formulation and execution together in the pursuit of corporate success and will be the subject of the last chapter.

Notes

1 A. De Groot. *Thought and Choice in Chess* (Amsterdam: Amsterdam University Press, 2008) (reprint).
2 A. De Groot. *Thought and Choice in Chess* (Amsterdam: Amsterdam University Press, 2008) (reprint).
3 A. De Groot. *Thought and Choice in Chess* (Amsterdam: Amsterdam University Press, 2008) (reprint).

Chapter 2

Strategic thinking

The importance of thinking

What does it mean to "think like a chess master"? Do corporate managers think, too, or does corporate life exclusively require operational skills?

This chapter stands out in a management book for its unconventional focus on philosophy, particularly cognitive psychology—the science of how the human mind thinks, or the science of strategic thinking. While we do not claim that a manager should be a philosopher, it is undeniable that thinking plays a vital role in an executive's responsibilities.

The question of "how we think" has always captivated philosophers throughout history. Although the ancient Greeks were unaware that the brain is the organ responsible for thinking—the heart was assumed to be the seat of intelligence and Aristotle believed that the brain was just a cooling mechanism for the blood—this did not stop them from developing the earliest theories on the subject. On one hand, Plato, with his theory of forms and idealism, was the first to explore the dynamics of abstract thinking. On the other hand, Aristotle emphasized empirical observation and categorized mental faculties such as perception, memory, and imagination, laying the groundwork for future cognitive theories. These contrasting views were masterfully depicted by Raphael in his painting "The School of Athens", where Plato is shown pointing upward (symbolizing idealism), while Aristotle points downward (representing realism).

It wasn't until the 19th century that the functions of certain brain areas were discovered through experiments on animals. These discoveries often involved vivisection or ablation of brain parts to observe the resulting functional impairments. Obviously, these invasive methods were not feasible for studying human cognition. And here is where chess emerged as a valuable, non-invasive tool for exploring the human mind.

DOI: 10.4324/9781003533719-2

The experiments on the chess champions' minds

In the '40s and the '50s of the 20th century, psychologist and chess player Adriaan de Groot carried out his famous experimental study on how chess champions think when they prepare their next move. During the tests, he showed the champions different chess positions, asking them to expose verbally their mental process when choosing a move. He then recorded their verbal accounts into structured protocols with the help of a team of psychologists. The comparative analysis of these protocols allowed de Groot to identify the categories of strategic thinking that laid the foundations of modern Strategic Management theories.[1]

de Groot's experiments were carried out within the theoretical framework of the non-associationist theory[2] which considered the human mind as a processing machine that implements different methods to solve a problem, to make a decision, or to define a new objective.

de Groot's experiments are entirely valid for a business environment once the following replacements are applied:

- Chess position -> business scenario
- Make a move -> make a decision
- Chess champion/grand master -> experienced manager
- Chess beginner -> junior business analyst

We will attempt to explain de Groot's results using the example of a newly appointed CEO's first days.

The General Assembly of New Energies Inc. has decided to appoint John Smith as the new CEO and has requested that he present a new company strategy within the first month of his appointment. As soon as John learns of his new role, even before the formal minutes of the Assembly are published, he begins preparing by reviewing publicly available materials, such as financial statements, sustainability reports, and press reviews. According to John, this initial research phase allows him to form a preliminary understanding of the company. This understanding is essentially a conceptual framework created through abstraction, which involves selecting a few key pieces of relevant information. This simplified yet sufficiently detailed framework will help John refine and develop a comprehensive strategy. This is what de Groot defines as the orientation phase where the faculty of abstraction plays a key role in elaborating a conceptual scheme of the situation which will be used to define a strategic objective.

However, John knows that this initial scheme is too rudimentary and needs refinement. Once he is officially appointed, he arranges a plenary meeting with the company's EVPs. During this meeting, he illustrates his preliminary idea of the company through some PowerPoint slides and collects feedback from the EVPs, with the PowerPoint slides serving as the visual and sharable representation of his mental scheme of the company.

After incorporating the information from the meeting, John believes that the scheme of the situation is now robust enough to manipulate in order to visualize a target scheme, which is the strategic objective to present to the shareholders. He begins to understand the current problems the company faces and visualizes the target situation as if those problems have been resolved. In de Groot's experiments, this visualization of the target situation is termed "schematic anticipation of the objective" and serves to highlight the gap between the current situation and the desired outcome.

John then convenes a second meeting with all the EVPs to test his vision of the future. During the meeting, he begins analyzing some of the options available to the company. After each analysis, he pauses to let his colleagues express their opinions. After listening to the EVPs' comments, John enters into an introspective reflection, his brow furrowed, his demeanor focused. This is what de Groot defines as a transition phase, a moment between two analysis phases that integrates the results of the recent analysis and prepares the mind for the next investigation. Similar to the orientation phase, the main activity here is abstraction rather than calculation. This special abstraction process aims to define a new problem-solving proposition to be explored. Relations and properties are abstracted and incorporated into the initial scheme of the problem. The result of a transitional phase is an improved systematization of the problem and a revision of expectations.

Transitional phases are typically brief and involve silence, passivity, and introspection rather than clear verbal expression. They are generally more pronounced when the result of an analysis phase is negative, when a crisis of expectations needs to be managed, or when a strongly favored option must be discarded. The typical characteristics of transition phases include returning to the primary high-level objective (big picture), integrating the results from the latest analysis phase, and often explicitly reformulating the scheme of the problem.

Once John has gathered feedback from the EVPs on all the options he had analyzed, he realizes it is time to make a final decision on the strategy to present to the shareholders.

Since the beginning of his approach to the new company, John had developed an unconscious preference for one particular option. So now, at the end of the process, he needs to demonstrate that this favorite option quantitatively dominates the cluster of all other options, while he instinctively knows that it is the one he would like to pursue, having previously managed a similar transaction in his professional experience. Therefore, he assigns the Chief Financial Officer (CFO) the task of preparing a financial assessment for all the options he presented during the meeting.

This final phase, known as the verification phase in de Groot's studies, occurs when it's time to wrap up. Here the process converges from a problem with multiple choices (as it was at the beginning) to a problem of choice between a favorite option and the cluster of all the other options grouped together. Here the chess player/corporate executive strives to demonstrate the superiority of the favorite move over all the other options.

The main mechanism involved in this process of convergence is clustering, i.e. grouping together a number of alternatives according to one or more characteristics. A strategy or a plan can be considered as a particular cluster of options. Clustering is a fast and efficient way to discard a large number of alternatives without spending time in analyses.

The formation of a favorite move is another mechanism to reduce the available options. This process starts during the orientation phase with a general impression, mainly related to intuition and a hint of emotional preference, but needs to be confirmed during the analysis phases. A favorite move is generally analyzed first and is characterized by a series of non-immediate re-investigations to prove its superiority.

A favorite option can emerge immediately in the initial phase of orientation (especially in tactical positions where an advantage can be achieved in a few steps) or later in the process with a step-by-step convergence. A favorite move can be changed only after a "crisis of expectations" i.e. a drastic negative deviation from expectations.

The recapitulation or verification phase ends with the elaboration of a *subjectively convincing qualitative argument.* In most cases, this argument is objectively incomplete and contains an intuitive and emotional expectation to compensate for the practical impossibility of an exhaustive analysis.

Therefore two conditions must be met before we can make a decision:

1 The favorite move must quantitatively dominate all other alternatives, as a result of the analysis phases
2 The qualitative argument must be subjectively convincing

Regarding the first point, we saw that John assigned the CFO the task to prepare a financial assessment of all the available options.

As for the second point, John was aware that he had an instinctively preferred one particular option since the beginning of the process, having previously managed a similar transaction in his professional experience.

Through the tale of John's settlement in the new position, we have seen how de Groot identified four types of stages in the process of making a decision: orientation phase, analysis phases, transition phases, and verification phase.[3] I suggest renaming these four phases based on their induced physical reactions, aiming to make them easier to remember:

1 Orientation phase -> Adrenalin phase, due to the stress resulting from the gap identified between the current and target situation
2 Analysis phases -> "Sweat and blood" phases, due to the mental energies consumed in the analyses of the available options
3 Transition phases -> "Furrowed brow" phases, due to the mental effort to integrate the results of the just-concluded analysis phase into the initial scheme of the problem
4 Verification phase -> "Relief and reward" phase, due to the satisfaction of having successfully come to the conclusion of the decision-making process

The adrenaline phase

In the initial stage, often referred to as the "orientation phase", the decision-maker assesses the situation and forms a general idea of what to do next, creating a mental image of the objective—a vision of the solved problem, called a schematic anticipation of the objective in de Groot's studies. For instance, a chess player might visualize a desired board position, while a manager envisions a successful business scenario. This mental anticipation highlights the gap between the current situation and the desired outcome, generating a sense of tension. The body responds to this mental stress by releasing adrenaline, preparing for the upcoming decision-making process. The higher the gap identified, the higher the release of adrenaline.

The sweat and blood phases

The second stage, known as the "exploration or analysis phases", requires hard work to analyze options and calculate expected outcomes. de Groot's research on chess masters uncovered mechanisms like the widely recognized SWOT framework (strengths, weaknesses, opportunities, and threats),[4] a recurring tool for analyzing chess positions and market situations in MBA books. It involves:

- Preliminary assessment of the position.
- Static analysis of the relationships between the elements of the position.
- Dynamic analysis of possibilities for direct action.

de Groot noted that beginners tend to focus on the static evaluation, counting for example the pieces on the chessboard while champions would analyze perspective and dynamic plans, assessing resources (pieces) only when a plan has been chosen. de Groot also noted that beginners do not express value judgments and even at the end of the analysis process they hardly have a clear opinion on the position. Conversely, champions are very bold and self-confident in expressing their evaluations, even at the early stages of analysis.

Within the analysis phases, the organization of the thought process, in particular for the solution of complex problems, is hierarchical, based on progressive levels of deepening. Figure 2.1, derived from one of de Groot's protocols, shows us the levels of progressive deepening of the analysis with what and how much is calculated at each stage.[5] The tree structure represents the overall approach of the analysis, while the "filled" leaves are the options analyzed in each phase.

Among the analysis methods identified by de Groot are:

- The in-depth dialectic analysis, a method that can be traced back to Plato's dialogue "Protagoras". This process begins by questioning the initial judgment to highlight its weaknesses. Then, these weaknesses are themselves scrutinized to achieve a balanced evaluation of the position's pros and cons. A typical example of the implementation of this methodology is the hot chair technique. Let's assume we are planning a meeting with our leader in order to request a salary increase. Let's position two chairs one in front of the other. First, we would sit in one chair and present the supporting evidence for why we believe we deserve a raise. Then, we would switch to the opposite chair, adopting the perspective of our leader, and challenge the evidence we just presented. Finally, we would return to our original chair and counter our leader's objections. By the end of this process, we would have developed very strong arguments that already address potential objections, making them almost irrefutable.

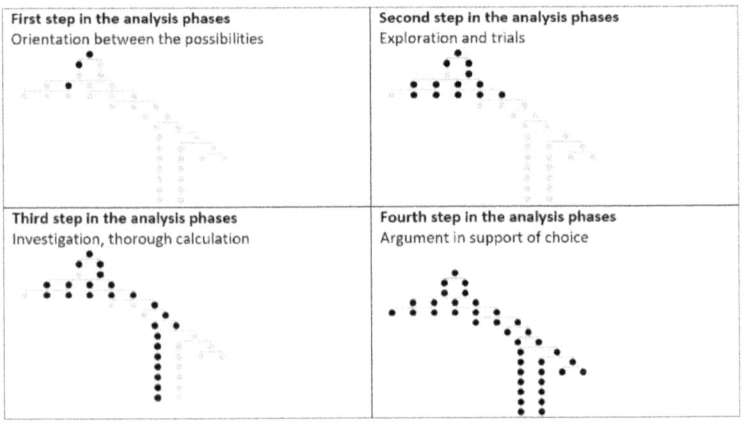

Figure 2.1 Progressive deepening in the analysis phases

- The method of stand-by often referred to as the method of "no move, what can the opponent do?" is useful to investigate the enemy's strengths and threats.
- The method of proceeding by trial and error, often referred to as empirical investigation. It involves systematic experimentation rather than random attempts. These trials take place within a predefined realm of possibilities shaped by the schematic anticipation of the objective. Proceeding by trial and error offers numerous advantages:
    - It may result in finding a direct solution to the problem
    - It is an exploratory means which increases the information on the problem
    - It may result in the discovery of new solution methods

One last mechanism highlighted by de Groot in these phases involves re-investigations, i.e. moves that, although discarded in a previous phase, may be revisited. This process is known as the re-investigations of the same solution proposition. When presented with options A, B, C, D, etc., each can be evaluated and categorized sequentially, for instance:

C—B—A—C—D—A—A—D—B—......, where A has been re-investigated three times, while B twice.

The cycle of revisiting plans or moves, even those initially discarded, is often mistaken for hesitation or lack of resolve. In reality, re-evaluating discarded options happens within a new context enriched by the deeper understanding and insights gained from exploring other possibilities. The recommendation that this process should not be confused with indecision or a lack of determination is proven by de Groot's studies where both beginners and chess champions show a similar average frequency of re-investigations, highlighting its important role within the strategic thinking process.

However, readers should be cautious not to excessively revisit the same options, as this can quickly deplete limited and valuable mental energy.

Finally, it is worth mentioning that toward the conclusion of the decision-making process, re-investigations tend to occur more frequently and play a crucial role in solidifying the rationale for the decision being considered.

The frowned brow phases

The transition between two analysis phases is marked by a transitional phase whose function is to integrate the results of the preceding analyses and prepare the mind for the next investigation. Unlike calculation-heavy stages, these phases involve abstraction, aiming at formulating new solutions. Relations and properties are abstracted and included in the initial problem's scheme, contributing to the progress of the problem and its solution. These phases are typically brief and involve introspection, especially when managing a crisis of expectations or when discarding a favored move. The focus returns to the high-level schematic anticipation of the objective, integrating the latest analysis results, and often reformulating the problem.

The relief and reward phase

Finally, in the fourth stage, called the verification phase, the process converges from a problem with multiple choices (as it was at the beginning) to a problem of choice between a favorite move and the cluster of all the other moves grouped together. This convergence involves clustering alternatives and forming a favorite move, initially based on intuition and emotional preference, and confirmed during analysis. A favorite move might emerge immediately in tactical positions (where we know what we need to do) or later through step-by-step convergence. Changes from a favorite option to a new favorite one can happen but only when a significant deviation from expectations occurs. This final verification phase ends with the formulation of a subjectively convincing qualitative argument, usually combining objective analysis with intuitive and emotional expectations.

To make a decision, two conditions must be met:

- The favorite move must quantitatively dominate all other alternatives.
- The qualitative argument must be subjectively convincing.

Let's illustrate these conditions with two examples, one from chess and one from business:

- In chess: "I'll play Nb1-c3 (Knight from b1 to c3) because it's better than the alternatives (quantitative argument) and helps me prepare an attack (qualitative argument)".
- In business: "I'll buy company X for its technology (qualitative argument) as development would be more expensive (quantitative argument)".

When options have similar quantitative evaluations, the final decision usually depends on personal preferences or emotions, a topic explored further in the next chapter on decision-making.

Regarding de Groot's process of strategic thinking, Figure 2.2 outlines the main mechanisms identified in each phase.

Within de Groot's sequential decision-making process, some of the most interesting results involve the interaction between the roles of abstraction and experience. While experience is highly regarded in the business community, abstraction is probably the most underestimated and neglected management skill. However as we could already appreciate in

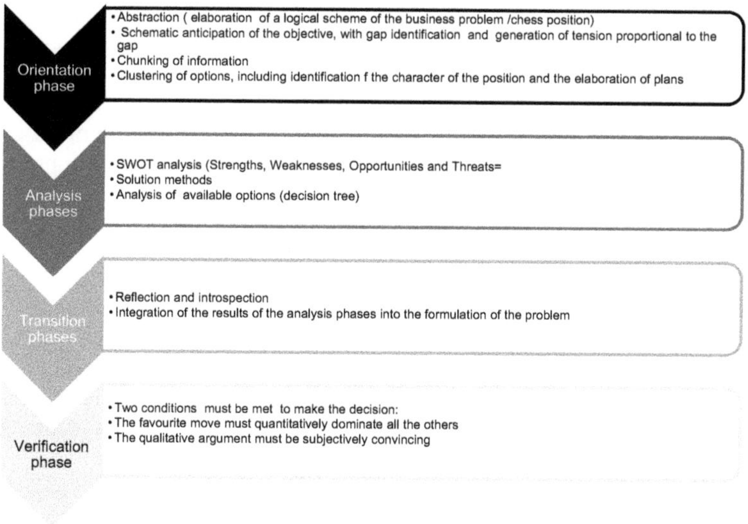

Figure 2.2 Summary of de Groot's process of strategic thinking

the introductive chapter, abstraction plays a fundamental role in elaborating the scheme of reality which will be the starting point to solve a problem, to make a decision, or to define a strategic objective. In order for managers to better visualize the importance of this function, we should look at it as the ability to prepare effective high-level PowerPoint schemes of the problem including all and only the necessary details, the so-called big picture.

In the following paragraphs, we will examine in detail the roles of abstraction and experience, two contrasting mechanisms that, in a sense, echo the divergent perspectives of Plato and Aristotle on cognitive psychology, *si parva licet componere magnis*.

Experience or the champion's arsenal

When selecting a candidate for a senior role, the experience is the standard criterion.

In military terms, experience is often referred to by the more evocative expression, "the champion's arsenal". It's no surprise that corporate leaders, much like chess champions, take pride in their own arsenal—a collection of tactical and strategic weapons they've developed over years of practice and study. These weapons can be called upon to win in situations that resemble challenges they've faced before.

In our approach, the arsenal consists of all the schemes and patterns the champion has accumulated through experience.

In cognitive terms, the building blocks of the champion's arsenal were identified in 1973 by Chase and Simon, who supported de Groot's findings in their book "Perception in Chess".[6] Their initial objective was to explore the dynamics of short-term memory by comparing the performances of chess champions and beginners. In their experiments, the exposure to the chess position was shorter than in de Groot's. When chess champions observed a position for five seconds, they could reproduce it with remarkable accuracy. In contrast, under the same conditions, beginners could only reproduce a few pieces. This gap cannot be explained solely by champions' higher mnemonic capacity, as it disappears in random positions, where both champions and beginners could only reproduce a few pieces. The superior performance of strong players is attributed to their ability to encode the position into broader "perceptual blocks" or chunks, each representing a familiar sub-configuration of pieces, that uses up limited memory resources. For example, castling can be seen as an effortless chunk that encompasses the positions of six pieces (the King, one Rook, and three pawns).

The number of chunks stored by our short-term memory after a quick exposure to a chess position is comparable to our immediate recollection of common words or visual patterns. Champions are better at reconstructing a position due to their repertoire of methods of play (chunks) developed through experience and study: the so-called *champion's arsenal*. The champion in fact "sees" in a few seconds which method of play is more appropriate for the situation at hand and directs the investigation in a highly specific direction, while the beginner is still immersed in the phase of counting the number of pieces. The expression "it's only a matter of technique" is frequently used when the champions recognize a scheme from the repertoire of their own experience and know exactly the outcome of the application of that scheme.

The champions or the experienced managers are such because of the experience that they have accumulated over the years in terms of highly specialized perception modes and reproductively available analytical methods.

Finally, as Ukrainian-born American chess writer Irving Chernev once remarked, "Every chess master was once a beginner", which is a point worth remembering.

The faculty of abstraction

Abstraction involves selecting pertinent information necessary to achieve an objective while disregarding less critical details. This process results in schematizing the objective or constructing a mental map. While not diminishing the importance of this function, managers should view it as the skill to swiftly create mental PowerPoint charts outlining the situation.

de Groot's experiments offer a compelling illustration of the mechanisms of abstraction. In one protocol, chess players were tasked with reproducing a position after viewing it for only ten seconds. The resulting

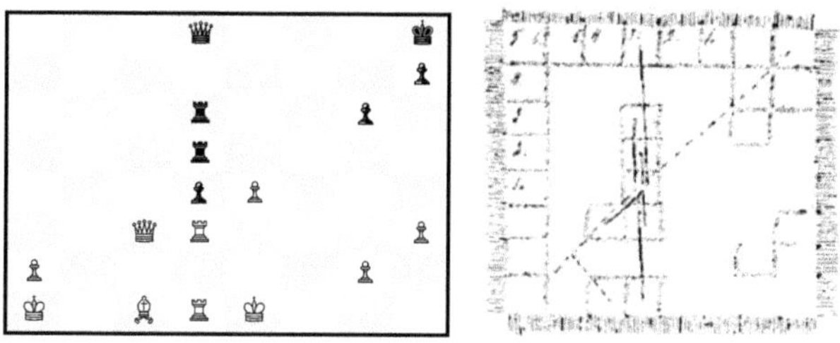

Figure 2.3 de Groot's example of abstraction[7]

data, as shown in Figure 2.3.[8] demonstrate how the position was simplified into a mental scheme based on logical relationships between pieces. The specific arrangement of pieces on the chessboard was deemed irrelevant.

Abstraction is the initial cognitive process triggered when encountering a novel problem. This activation occurs rapidly, typically within seconds, and involves two distinct phases:

1 Recalling one or more schemes from the "champion's arsenal" that potentially represent the current position accurately.
2 Analyzing the differences between the actual position and the recalled scheme. This comparison allows to direct the focus of analysis efforts exclusively toward the identified differences. Managing all other aspects of the position is implicitly guided by the recalled scheme.

When a chess champion (or manager) says, "What stands out to me in this position are two things...", they are drawing on their experience to recognize a familiar scheme and identify two specific aspects that deviate from it. These two deviating elements then become the primary focus of further analysis. In contrast, chess beginners and junior managers often waste energy analyzing in multiple directions without the advantage of an experienced-based framework.

Out of sheer curiosity, the inverse function of abstraction is *tachistoscopy,* a cognitive process that allows individuals to perceive or understand patterns or images from abstract representations without needing to go through extensive analysis or detail-oriented examination. Tachistoscopy is a distinctly human function that is difficult for computers to replicate. This capability lies at the heart of protective software designed to prevent malware programs from automatically accessing specific websites.

Figure 2.4 illustrates common examples of tachistoscopy often encountered while navigating the Internet.

They are both examples of a CAPTCHA, short for "Completely Automated Public Turing test to tell Computers and Humans Apart". This test is

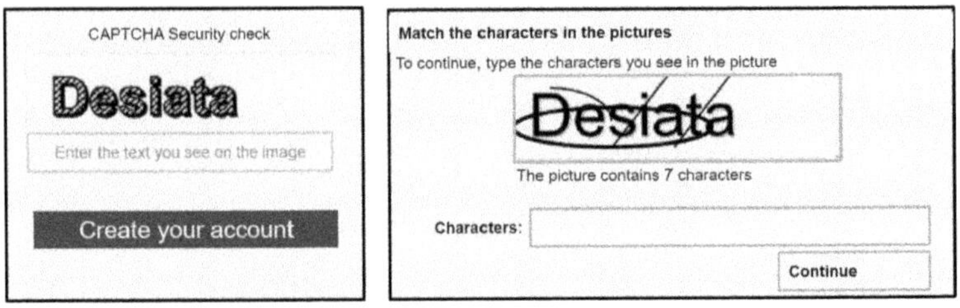

Figure 2.4 Examples of CAPTCHA

employed on the Internet to ascertain whether the user is human, relying on a uniquely human cognitive ability. We will revisit this concept when discussing neural networks in the chapter focused on decision-making.

Conclusions

The most remarkable aspect of the vast complexity of the mental process analyzed by de Groot is how effortlessly and smoothly the human mind handles it. In de Groot's studies, even the least experienced beginners never "lose the thread". The progression and evolution of the problem unfold in an organized manner, without hesitation or the need to recall where we are in the process.

Therefore, it appears that the problem-solving structure of a complex problem is an innate function of the human mind, regardless of the player's skill level or the manager's experience. Contrary to common assumptions, de Groot's studies convincingly demonstrate that top chess champions are not superhuman computers. Surprisingly, their depth of analysis is comparable to that of beginners: both champions and beginners typically analyze 40–50 nodes in a decision tree before making a move. The difference lies in the champions' superior ability to recognize standard patterns within a position. This ability stems from their extensive repertoire of game patterns developed through experience and study—the so-called "champion's arsenal". Indeed, champions can "see" within moments a strategic approach best suited to the situation. They immediately focus their investigation on specific operational directions (thoroughly analyzing the correct variations and promptly dismissing poor moves), whereas a beginner may still be preoccupied with simply counting the number of pieces on the board.

de Groot's research suggests that "champions are made, not born", a principle that clearly extends to corporate leaders as well. We all share the same inherent predisposition and mental structure for tackling complex problems. Yet, to fully leverage this potential, it is essential to develop a comprehensive "champion's arsenal" through years of commitment, learning, perseverance, and passion.

Chapter 2 Strategic thinking—interviews

Luca Desiata, interviewed by Bachar Kouatly

Q.: This chapter started with a citation of Plato's and Aristotle's ideas. What do you think about philosophy in the Corporate World?

A.: I believe that the corporate world incorporates much more philosophy than is commonly recognized. Historically, the organization of work and labor has inspired deep philosophical reflection to frame industrial production systems, including classical liberalism, Marxism, Taylorism, Fordism, and Just-in-Time.

This pertains to philosophical systems related to the external environment in which the corporation operates.

Shifting the focus to the internal environment of the corporation where people live and work, we can find philosophy in the following fields: ethics and Corporate Social Responsibility which define the constructive impact of the company within the broader society; occupational psychology concerning employees' well-being and motivation; cognitive psychology related to managers' decision-making processes as illustrated in this chapter; and the role of logic in computer science, and the role of mathematics and statistics in finance.

Q.: Which step in de Groot's processes resonated the most with you?

A.: I was particularly intrigued by a seemingly minor finding: the strategy of "no move, what can the opponent do", which reminded me of the art of playing the waiting game, successfully implemented by the Roman general Fabio Massimo against Hannibal.

Another mechanism that resonates with my experience is the distinction between chess amateurs and champions, particularly this finding related to counting versus not counting the pieces on the board: the champion in fact "sees" in a few seconds which method of play is more appropriate for the situation at hand and directs the investigation in a highly specific direction, while the beginner is still immersed in the phase of counting the number of pieces.

This reflects my own professional evolution. As a young strategy consultant around 25 years ago, my role in organizational assessments involved counting resources in each organizational function of the client, which would then help shape the overall strategy crafted by the senior partner in the consulting team. However, in 2016 when I became CEO of Sogin, I immediately "saw" what needed to be done without even knowing the exact number of employees. Only after establishing a strategic objective would I assess the available resources to achieve it.

What aspect of cognitive psychology are you most skeptical about?

I must say that I fully agree with every finding in de Groot's study. The validity of his conclusions is evidenced by the advancements in computer technology that he inspired. However, I strongly disagree with the opposite approach proposed by the founders of NLP (Neuro-Linguistic Programming). Unlike de Groot's idea of exploring the human mind's fascinating mechanisms to replicate and enhance them with machines, NLP suggests that the human mind can be reprogrammed and remodeled just like a computer. I was honestly relieved when I read that NLP has been labeled as a pseudoscientific approach to cognitive psychology due to the lack of scientific evidence supporting its principles.

Q.: As a chess player what is your personal experience between chess and cognitive functions?

A.: I have actively utilized chess to assess my cognitive abilities. This assessment became particularly crucial following a stroke I experienced in 2020, which left a hole in my cortex. I was concerned that this could affect my mental acuity. Immediately after the ischemic attack, my speech was confused my thoughts unclear, so I was understandably very worried. Fortunately, as evidenced by my historical performances on a well-known online chess platform, this has not been the case. I ended up in a wheelchair, half paralyzed, but my main concerns were about my mental sharpness rather than mobility, in full alignment with Italian Nobel Prize winner Rita Levi Montalcini's famous saying "Let the body do what it pleases. I am the mind".

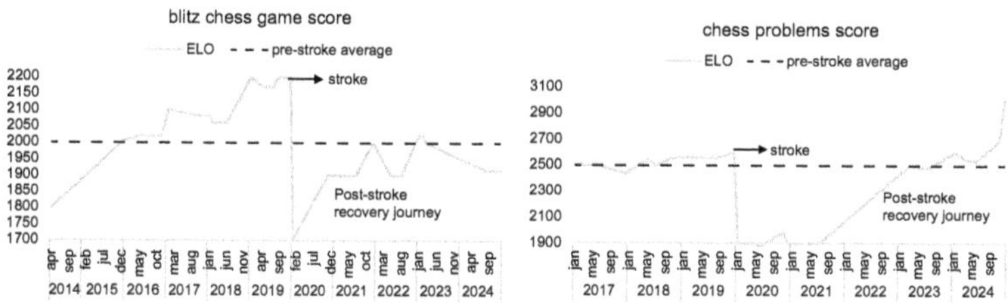

Figure 2.5 Author's chess performance before and after stroke

Regarding cognitive strength, the first chart on the left illustrates my performance in blitz chess games (where each player has only five minutes to finish the game), a highly stressful format with limited time for each move. The chart shows that my cognitive strength has significantly improved since the stroke, although it has not yet fully recovered.

The chart on the right in Figure 2.5 displays my performance in chess problem-solving, a more relaxed format with ample time to analyze and find the best move. This chart shows that my performance in this specific field is even above pre-stroke levels, indicating that I have fully recovered in situations without external pressure (Figure 2.5).

In conclusion, my mind operates perfectly despite the cortical lesion. Chess has served as a reassuring, objective measure to affirm this statement.

A few weeks after the stroke, I required surgery to place two stents in my left carotid artery to protect it and prevent the dissection that had occurred on the right side of my neck, which had led to the ischemic attack. Although the surgery was not particularly risky, the surgeon asked me to signal if I felt myself losing consciousness. Given the paradoxical nature of this request (if I lost consciousness, how could I inform the medical team?), I suggested playing a blindfolded chess game with the anesthesiologist during the procedure. This allowed them to monitor my brain's status simply by listening to my voice as I played chess with one of the doctors.

Anatoly Karpov, interviewed by Bachar Kouatly

Chess champions are perceived by the public opinion as strategic thinking machines, endowed with superhuman qualities. Is it true?

I hope not to disappoint the readers, but I believe that, contrary to popular belief, chess champions are very ordinary people whose only distinction is that their professional lives are entirely absorbed by the highly intellectual nature of chess. The portrayal of chess masters as extraordinary thinkers is a creation of the media. To generate compelling news for the general public, journalists often emphasize the more unusual aspects of chess masters' behavior (Morphy's madness,[9] for example, or Fischer's eccentric behavior and mental health problems)[10] as if some kind of strangeness were the natural consequence of deep mental concentration and complex analyses.

Chess champions find satisfaction and joy in their passion for the game, without needing or seeking formal recognition. Take the case of Russian mathematician Grigori Perelman, for example. In 2006, he was awarded the prestigious Fields Medal—often considered the Nobel Prize of mathematics—for his exceptional work in differential geometry. To the astonishment of the scientific community, he declined the medal. To me, this decision was understandable; he chose to forgo fame, honor, and worldly accolades to retreat to his hometown and immerse himself in the intellectual pleasures he values.

While I wouldn't go to the extremes of Perelman, I certainly share his appreciation for intellectual beauty and the joys of the mind. I have managed to balance these pleasures with a fulfilling life: I have a family, work as a parliament member at the Russian Duma, and have interests and friends beyond the world of chess. However, I must admit that during the world championship against Kasparov, the level of tension was so intense that I felt disconnected from the world. There was no room for other interests or distractions—chess consumed every moment, day and night, like an obsession. The extreme pressure of such events could easily lead to unconventional and impulsive behavior, which the press was quick to exaggerate and idealize for public consumption.

Are you familiar with de Groot's experiments?

de Groot's experiments are well known in the chess community although they only circulate in an extremely simplified popularization proposed by some commentators. I am sure that few people have read the whole treatise, due to its complicated structure filled with statistical analyses, psychological assumptions, and chess technicalities. The original version is therefore hardly usable while I found very interesting the summary provided in the *Chess and Corporate Strategy* book because it condenses in layman's language the key messages of interest for a wide audience, not necessarily limited to chess players or managers.

What do you think of the results of the experiments?

Although the experiments were conducted on great chess champions from the last century (such as Euwe), I believe that the mechanisms of strategic thinking have remained unchanged. In fact, I would argue that they are applicable across various areas of life, not just in chess and business. I agree with de Groot's overall approach, but I think the thought process occurs on a conscious level in a more intuitive and less mechanical manner than he described. When evaluating a new chess position, I quickly identify the strategic issues, advantages and disadvantages, and potential strong moves. Clearly, years of experience and practice are crucial in reaching this level. After the initial phase of assessing the position, I focus on achieving harmony and coordination among the pieces, exploring possible opportunities. Only at the end of this process do I calculate move sequences to verify or adjust the conclusions drawn in the first phase.

Is there anything that you do not share?

The conclusion I find challenging to accept is that champions and beginners are comparable in terms of memory skills and computational abilities. I agree with Chase and Simon that recalling the exact position of pieces in random games is difficult because the logical relationships that provide meaning and help organize the position in our memory are absent. Nevertheless, I am convinced that I possess an exceptional memory, even for random chess positions, which exceeds the average.

One swallow does not make a summer, but chess history does feature notable instances of hypermnesia or extraordinary memory. For example, Tal[11] is renowned for his remarkable ability to recall an entire page of text after just a brief glance, even years later. While I have great respect for psychologists and their research, I believe that all top chess players possess some form of exceptional memory skill. The real question is determining the extent to which these abilities are innate versus developed through practice.

With regard to the computational power and the parity with beginners, it is true that the champion directs the analysis in a very specific direction from the very beginning making the process efficient. But, even in this case, I am convinced that with practice and motivation, anybody can develop above-the-average computational skills, just like any sportsman in their field.

How has the approach to chess evolved since the time when de Groot conducted his experiments?

Certainly, the style of play has evolved. No one today would attempt the daring and romantic sacrifices that were popular in the 19th century. The vast accumulation of knowledge over centuries has refined the tactics and strategies available to champions, enhancing defensive techniques and reducing the impact of reckless attacks. Even Tal, who initially made his mark with a notably romantic style, eventually recognized the need to bolster his technical and defensive skills to remain competitive against more sophisticated positional players.

How have computers impacted the game?

Computers have transformed several key aspects of strategic thinking. For instance, they have removed the psychological element, which was and continues to be crucial in determining victory in high-level human competitions. Computers have also altered the concept of "purpose". Before the rise of artificial intelligence, it was unthinkable for a human player to make a move outside of a predefined plan, as demonstrated by de Groot. In chess, it's traditionally said that "every move must have a purpose". However, computers have shown that a move can be played without a specific plan, with its merit being judged simply by the absence of clear short-term or long-term disadvantages.

On one hand, computers have greatly expanded our understanding of chess. On the other hand, they have made the game more mechanical, diminishing the role of imagination and intuition. For instance, the 2011 world champion Anand, who heavily relies on advanced computers for his preparation, has a playing style that I don't particularly enjoy. I recall his match against Topalov in Corsica in 2003, where Anand played the move 11… Kh5 (Knight to h5). This move seemed more characteristic of a computer program like Fritz than a human player. Human logic would typically dismiss such a move, as it immediately results in the loss of a pawn. In contrast, a computer would analyze it as just another option, considering the possibility of recovering the pawn later in the game. This suggests to me that Anand's analytical process may closely resemble that of a computer.

Is the process of strategic thinking in chess the same in a real game, a problem, or a study?

Completely different!

A chess composition is a work of pure beauty, designed to showcase a clear theme. In contrast to the energy and intensity of a real game, aesthetic and contemplative elements take precedence. It comes down to personal preference: the serene appreciation of beauty and meditation versus the dynamic and unpredictable nature of a competitive game.

The mindset required to find a solution also differs: in a chess problem or study, we know the outcome with certainty (such as checkmate in two moves), whereas, in a game, we can never be completely certain about the value of the position.

A third difference between the two approaches lies in the quality and quantity of experience that each player develops over time, tailored to their specific focus in chess—whether competition or composition. While these experience patterns share the common foundation of chess rules, they are not interchangeable and evolve in different directions based on their objectives.

How does chess strategic thinking relate to the era in which it evolved?

I believe that every historical period influences chess strategic thinking in a profound way.

During the Renaissance, when Rome and Florence dominated global culture and commerce, the world's strongest players were Italian. In the 18th and mid-19th centuries, during the Napoleonic era, this supremacy shifted to the French. Then the British, Germans, and Americans, with few exceptions. In 1972, at the height of the Cold War, the titanic clash between the Russian champion Boris Spassky and the American challenger Bobby Fischer captivated the public's attention globally and became a metaphor for the Cold War itself. In 2012, in the wake of the emergence of the Asian economic powers, the male chess world champion was Indian and the female world champion was Chinese. These instances cannot be mere coincidences; chess mirrors the spirit of the times in which it develops.

Notes

1 A. De Groot. *Thought and Choice in Chess* (Amsterdam: Amsterdam University Press, 2008) (reprint).
2 On the opposite side, the associationist theory considers the mind as a black box and is best explained by the experiment on conditioned reflex and dog salivation carried out by the Russian physiologist Ivan Pavlov in the early 20th century.
3 A. De Groot. *Thought and Choice in Chess* (Amsterdam: Amsterdam University Press, 2008) (reprint).
4 A. De Groot. *Thought and Choice in Chess* (Amsterdam: Amsterdam University Press, 2008) (reprint).
5 A. De Groot. *Thought and Choice in Chess* (Amsterdam: Amsterdam University Press, 2008) (reprint).
6 W. G. Chase, H.A. Simon. Perception in Chess. *Cognitive Psychology*,Vol. 4, no. 1 (January 1973), pp. 55–81.
7 Chessboard drawn using Unicode chess pieces by piliapp.com
8 A. De Groot. *Thought and Choice in Chess* (Amsterdam: Amsterdam University Press, 2008) (reprint).
9 Paul Morphy (1837–1884) is widely regarded as the first unofficial world champion. He suffered of severe depression during the last years of his life.

10 Bobby Fischer is the only American-born world champion. He won the title in 1972, beating the Soviet champion Boris Spassky in a match compared to the "Cold War" between the two superpowers that the players represented. His extravagant behavior and his solitary private life, his poor social skills and obsession for the study of chess, led many psychologists to think that he suffered of a syndrome similar to autism.

11 Mikhail Tal became world champion in 1960 when he was just 24 years old. He was also known as "The Wizard of Riga" for his romantic style and his spectacular attacks.

Chapter 3

Decision-making

To underscore the importance of decision-making skills for managers, a survey by the strategy consultancy Bain reveals that companies excelling at making and executing strategic decisions demonstrate stronger financial performance.[1]

On the other hand, chess has been referred to as the drosophila of decision-making, drawing a parallel to the small fly that has significantly contributed to scientific advancements in biology and genetics. Chess serves as an ideal laboratory for testing decision-making strategies, as the outcome of the game provides an objective measure of the quality of each decision.

This love affair between chess and decision-making/artificial intelligence (AI) began at the dawn of theoretical computer science when Alan Turing developed Turochamp in 1948, the first algorithm designed to play chess (discussed further in the paragraph "situations of certainty" of this chapter). This foundational chess algorithm was too sophisticated for the hardware of the time and could only be executed manually.

Throughout the 20th century, chess remained a primary testing ground for AI. However, it is unclear whether scientists overstated the benefits of chess in computer science merely to justify using the most powerful computers of the time to spend hours playing their favorite game instead of working. This is what happened for example with the Daly CP chess program developed by NASA in 1970, whose primary scope was to entertain astronauts during their space missions. The fascination of these chess games in space inspired Stanley Kubrick, an avid chess player, to feature astronaut Frank Poole playing against the supercomputer HAL 9000's AI in his 1968 science fiction film "2001: A Space Odyssey". Kubrick's vivid imagination predicted the shocking computer-inflicted defeat of a human champion about 30 years before it actually happened.

Indeed, chess-playing software made substantial advancements in those years, culminating in IBM's Deep Blue system that defeated the reigning chess world champion Garry Kasparov in a six-game match in 1997. Despite suspicions of human intervention behind some of Deep

DOI: 10.4324/9781003533719-3

Blue's moves, its power primarily relied on brute force—a superior ability to calculate moves (up to 20 moves ahead in certain positions) coupled with an extensive database of opening positions and endgames. No human brain could ever match any of these capabilities.

While Kasparov's defeat prompted journalists and the intelligentsia to proclaim the end of human intelligence, computer science continued to advance in the following years. The significant leap forward came with the adoption of neural networks in AI systems, which we will explore in the first paragraph, while the rest of the chapter will focus on early decision-making techniques, which were characterized by intriguing and suggestive names like quiescence research, alpha-beta pruning, Minimax, decision trees, random decision forests, etc.

Before moving on to the next chapter, let's correct a partially inaccurate historical detail and recognize that the first chess-playing system was not Turing's algorithm but rather the so-called Mechanical Turk—a life-sized chess robot dressed as a sultan, leaning on a table with a chessboard (see Figure 3.1). Created in the 18th century by Wolfgang von Kempelen, it operated for over 80 years, captivating audiences as it toured European courts and American venues.

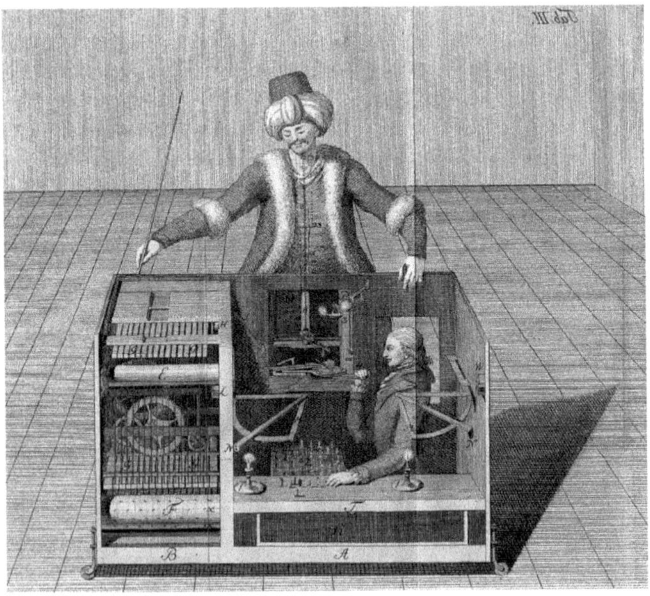

Figure 3.1 The Turk—By Joseph Racknitz—Humboldt University Library, Public Domain

It was only after its destruction by fire that it was revealed to be a hoax, operated by a human hidden inside.

A more serious effort at creating an autonomous chess-playing machine resulted in "El Ajedrecista" (Spanish for "The Chess Player"). Constructed in 1912 in Madrid, this device could correctly play the simple endgame of King and Rook versus King. It is considered the first real chess-playing computer and algorithm in history. Remarkably, it is still operational and is displayed at the Museo Torres Quevedo in the Escuela de Ingenieros de Caminos, Canales y Puertos in Madrid.

After this historical detour, let's return to more substantial matters and delve into the contemporary and captivating topic of neural networks.

Neural networks

The primary goal of AI is to recognize and interpret patterns or schemes, such as images, chess positions, or natural language processing. While this task is effortlessly handled by the human mind due to its faculties of abstraction and tachistoscopy, it has proven to be extremely complex for AI. Neural networks have been developed specifically to mimic the human mind's ability to recognize patterns and schemes.

So let's start with an easy task: recognize vertical segments in a 4 pixel × 4 pixel grid. This task is easy even for software and we do not need to train a neural network. We can just feed the system with all the possible configurations of vertical segments in the given grid. For every column, we have a total of six possible vertical segments (three 1-unit segments, two 2-unit segments, one 3-unit segment). Therefore, all the possible configurations of vertical segments in the 4 × 4 grid are 6 configurations per column, as shown in Figure 3.2. Six configurations per column × four columns = 24 possible configurations.

In this simple case, the input image, represented by a string of 0–1 values, is compared against the 0–1 strings of all possible vertical lines (see Figure 3.3). If a match is found, the output will be "it is a vertical line".

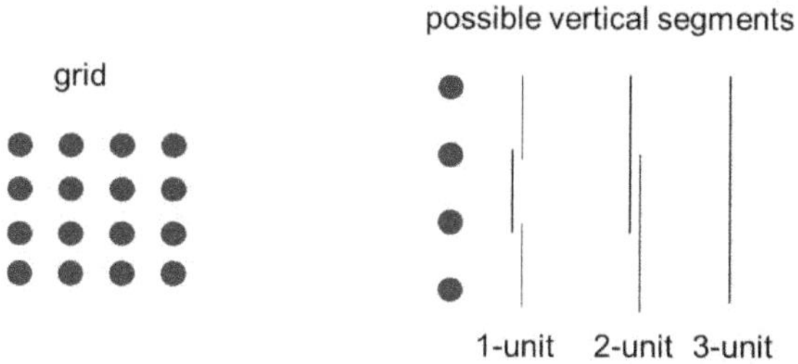

Figure 3.2 Vertical segments in a 4 × 4 grid

This case was so simple that one of the earliest applications, the barcode was patented in 1952.

Instead, if we consider a slightly more intricate task, such as recognizing handwritten letters, the system necessitates a significant increase in complexity as we cannot feed it with all possible ways in which letters can be drawn. Let's consider the letter A as an example (see Figure 3.4).

For human minds recognizing all images in Figure 3.4 as the letter A is a trivial task while, for image recognition software, it is very challenging and was impossible until a couple of decades ago. That is why letters with blurred borders or confusing lines often appear in CAPTCHA prompts, like the two in Figure 3.5.

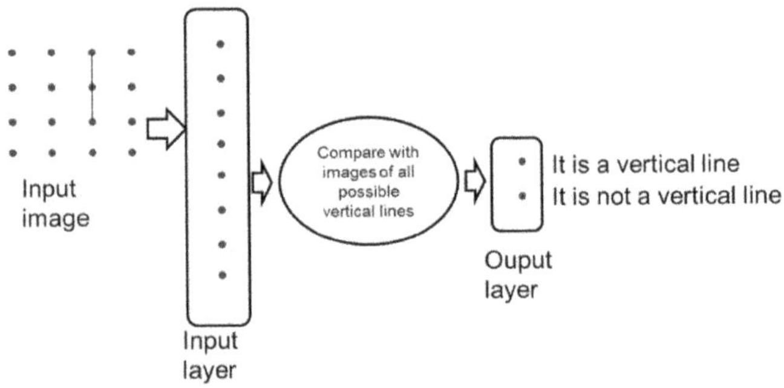

Figure 3.3 Is the input image a vertical line?

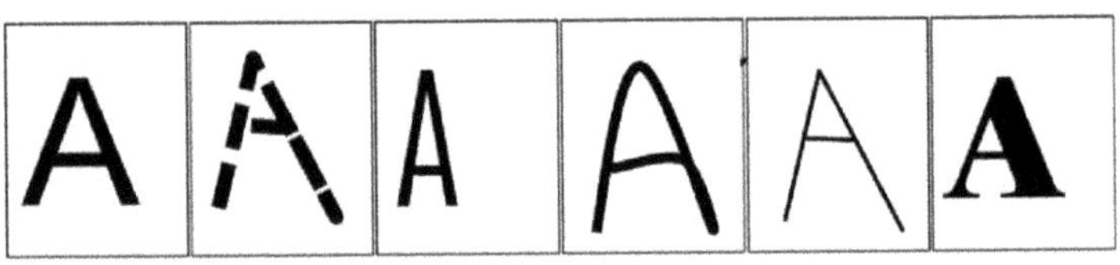

Figure 3.4 Letters A

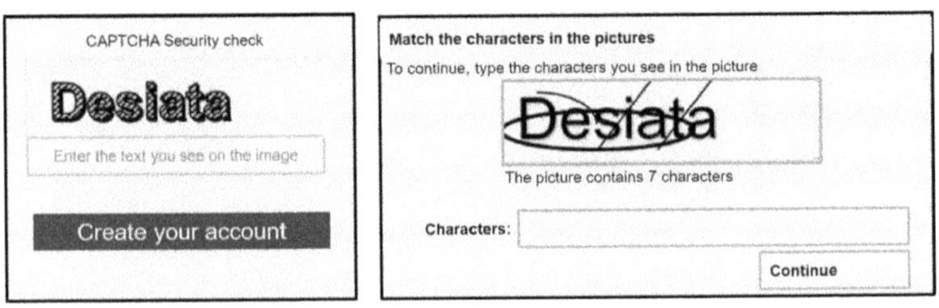

Figure 3.5 Examples of CAPTCHA

It is hard to believe that this recognition mechanism can be so challenging even for hackers. In fact, it has become the global gold standard for preventing malware from accessing websites.

So, let's attempt to break it down using neural networks.

Let's assume our grids with A letters (f) are 100 pixels × 100 pixels. Black pixels will be identified with 1, and white pixels with 0. Therefore, the input file will be a sequence of 0–1s depending on the chosen image.

The intriguing aspect of neural networks is their ability to identify patterns within an image, through the use of matrices of coefficients that are not visually interpretable. In contrast, humans recognize patterns as organized sub-components, such as three lines intersecting at various angles resulting in the letter A. Figure 3.6 represents the human way of identifying patterns for the letter A:

For the neural network, we'll define a neuron as a unit holding a number 0 or 1 with 1 for a black pixel and 0 for a white pixel. Neurons are organized in layers. The input layer is a vector of neurons representing the input image as a string of 0s and 1s; let's assume it has "m" neurons, with m = 10,000 for a 100 pixel × 100 pixel grid. The output layer is the answer we are looking for: Is it a letter A or not? In between there are one or more hidden layers performing the calculations to formulate the answer. Let's assume only one hidden layer with "n" neurons (see Figure 3.7).

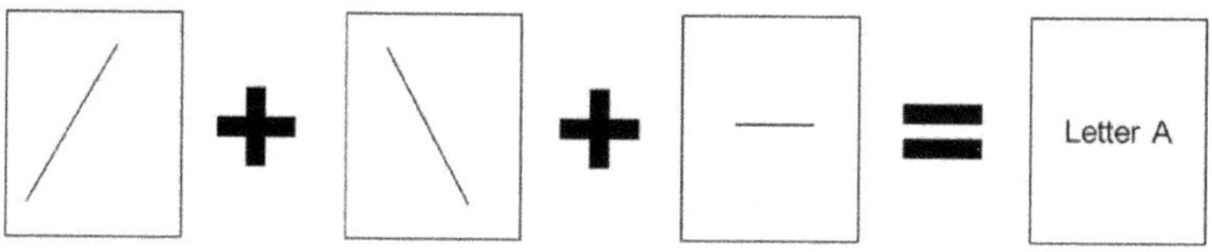

Figure 3.6 Human way of identifying pattern for the letter A

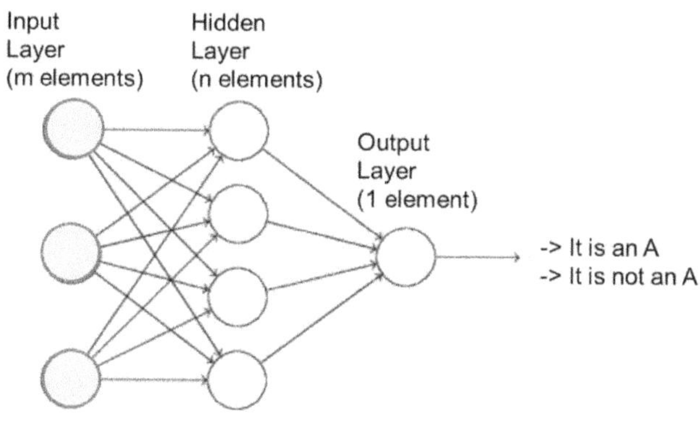

Figure 3.7 Layers of neurons

Neurons from the input layer will fire signals to the neurons of the hidden layer. Neurons in the hidden layer will be assigned a number 0 or 1 if the weighted sum of numbers in the input layer is below or above a certain threshold,[2] i.e. see Figure 3.8.

So, the values of the hidden layer will be as per Figure 3.9.

The value of the output layer will be given by another matrix that multiplies the values of the hidden layer.

At this point, we just need to feed the system with thousands of images of the letter A so that it can set the values in the matrices to give the correct answers. This phase is called the training of the neural network, aiming at determining the best set of coefficients in the matrices for maximizing the neural network's accuracy.

The unique aspect of chess compared to other pattern recognition tasks for neural networks is that during the training phase, chess does not necessarily require external data to teach the system to recognize chess patterns. Once the system is provided with the rules of the game, it can begin playing games by making random moves and assigning values of 0 or 1 to the output layer neurons depending on whether the game was won by Black or White. This approach mirrors the development path taken by one of the new generation engines, AlphaZero, which utilized a deep neural network (where deep means more than one hidden layer). While earlier engines relied on tree searches and databases of human-played games, AlphaZero autonomously mastered chess and quickly became the strongest chess software in the world. Despite remarkable progress in computational capacity, a complete solution for the game of chess remains elusive and is not expected to be found in the near future, if ever. The game's complexity is so vast that the number of possible chess positions (10^{120}) has been estimated by Claude Shannon in 1950[3] to exceed the number of atoms in the universe (10^{43}). As of today, only the game of

$$\text{Output} = \begin{cases} 0 \text{ if } \Sigma_j\, w_j\, x_j \leq \text{threshold} \\ 1 \text{ if } \Sigma_j\, w_j\, x_j > \text{threshold} \end{cases}$$

Figure 3.8 Values of the neurons in the hidden layer

$$\begin{bmatrix} Y1 \\ Y2 \\ \cdots \\ \cdots \\ \cdots \\ \cdots \\ Yn \end{bmatrix} = \begin{bmatrix} a_{11} & a_{12} & \cdots & a_{1n} \\ a_{21} & a_{22} & \cdots & a_{2n} \\ \cdots & \cdots & \cdots & \cdots \\ a_{m1} & a_{m2} & \cdots & a_{mn} \end{bmatrix} \times \begin{bmatrix} X_1 \\ X_2 \\ \cdots \\ \cdots \\ X_m \end{bmatrix}$$

Figure 3.9 Values of the neurons in the hidden layer

checkers with its 5×10^{20} positions has been solved. Perfect play by both sides leads to a draw.

AlphaZero's self-training in chess is reminiscent of Dr. B, the protagonist in Stefan Zweig's novella "The Royal Game" or "Schachnovelle".[4] After being arrested by the Gestapo and kept in complete isolation, Dr. B starts playing chess against himself, honing his ability to split his mind into two distinct personas. Over time, this leads him to gradually lose touch with reality. Hopefully, AI playing software will not meet the same fate.

Despite AlphaZero's remarkable achievements in chess, Moravec formulated a famous paradox about AI in 1988: "It is comparatively easy to make AI perform at an adult level on intelligence tests or playing checkers, but difficult or impossible to give them the skills of a one-year-old when it comes to perception and mobility".[5]

Classical decision-making methods

Decision-making is unquestionably the oldest human activity.

For those who argue that sex is humanity's oldest activity, it is important to highlight that since humans first appeared on Earth, the pursuit of sex led to the development of what is evolutionarily known as mating strategies. These strategies involve decision-making processes for identifying and selecting a sexual partner. Thus, decision-making predates sex in the historical timeline of human activities.

Decision-making has long been essential for human survival, dating back to our nomadic prehistoric ancestors. They had to determine the optimal times and locations for migration, as poor choices could lead to death by starvation or prolonged suffering. When confronted with excessive uncertainty and the weight of significant responsibility, the chieftain would seek guidance from the gods through an oracle or shaman. These spiritual advisors would determine the correct decision by interpreting ashes from a fire or employing other superstitious methods.

Fortunately for human survival, decision-making evolved into more sophisticated techniques. The ancient Persians, for instance, employed a two-pronged approach for important decisions. First, they would decide while heavily drunk, and then they would revisit the same decision when sober. If the two decisions matched, they considered it the right course of action. Alright, this may not be the best example of positive evolution in decision-making science. A better example comes from the Ancient Greeks and Romans, who perfected group decision-making skills to effectively manage their societies, e.g. the Roman senate or the institutions of the Greek polis.

Ancient times are also filled with anecdotes illustrating specific decision-making dilemmas, such as the legendary Dowry Dilemma.

The Dowry dilemma

Once upon a time, a sultan, knowing that his vizier was seeking a wife, decided to test the vizier's decision-making skills. He arranged for 100 women from his kingdom to be presented to the vizier one by one. The vizier's task was to choose the woman with the most substantial dowry. If he succeeded in selecting the richest candidate, he would keep his position and marry her; if he failed, he would be executed. The vizier could meet each woman individually, inquire about her dowry, and have to decide immediately whether to accept her or move on to the next, without the possibility of reconsidering previous candidates.

In addition to the longstanding social issue of the dowry system, which presents substantial challenges to gender equality and the empowerment of women, this ancient tale is an anecdotal variation of the decision-making problem of *optimal stopping*. The solution, elegant in its simplicity, calls for the rejection of the first n/e candidates (with n = total number of candidates and e = base of the natural logarithm) and then to choose the first next candidate whose dowry is higher than the discarded n/e. This rule provides a probability of 1/e= 37% to choose the best candidate and proves to be the best strategy starting from even small values of n. This means that the vizier should review 37 girls (100/e), remembering the highest dowry among the 37 (let us call it D), and then, starting from the 38th, choose the first candidate who has a dowry greater than D. In doing so, the vizier has a probability of 37% to choose the right lady.

Although it can be demonstrated that there is no best strategy, a probability of 63% for the vizier to be beheaded remains!

In decision-making theory, this story highlights the difficulty of solving the optimal stopping problem, which arises from the fact that our mental resources are finite, requiring a point where we must stop analyzing and taking action. This concept aligns with what De Groot termed the principle of economy of thought—the finite mental energy expended during decision-making, also known as decision fatigue. In the section on decision trees, we will explore additional techniques for identifying optimal stopping points.

Recognition-Primed Decision (RPD) process

The potentially prolonged process of the dowry dilemma starkly contrasts with the techniques used by managers and chess players, who must make quick decisions under conditions of uncertainty, incomplete information, and high pressure. In such scenarios, the RPD process comes into play, where you choose the first option that enables you to achieve the objective without breaching constraints. When faced with a problem, you generate a list of potential solutions based on your experience.

For each solution, you envision the course of action through imagination. If this mental simulation demonstrates that the objective can be achieved within the constraints, you opt for that solution without further consideration of alternatives.

In the upcoming paragraphs of this chapter, we will examine decision-making methodologies that have historically been refined through chess algorithms, specifically:

- Weighted average vote, a standard methodology in situations of certainty, where the alternatives, their outcomes, and the evaluation criteria are known;
- Decision trees, a standard methodology in problems with complex ramifications and in situations of uncertainty, where the outcomes depend on the environment, which is known in a probabilistic way;

Before examining these two decision-making methods, let's first explore a controversial technique that may appear farthest from the chess and corporate mindsets: flipping a coin.

Flipping a coin

Any rational agent, whether a chess player or manager, would be horrified at the proposal of tossing a coin to make a decision. This aversion stems from chess historically being seen as a symbol of intellect and will triumphing over fate, in stark contrast to dice, which represent chance and randomness. In a chess game, the outcome depends on the players' skill and the strength of their strategic plans. In contrast, rolling a die provides an equal probability of landing on any number from 1 to 6, regardless of the thrower's skill.

To reinforce this hypothesis of the rational player in chess, in 2008 during an interview on an Italian television channel, a journalist asked former world champion Garry Kasparov[6]:

"Is there a chance for me to beat you by making random moves to confuse you?"

Kasparov replied without hesitation:

"That's impossible. Randomness, the absence of strategy, guarantees a 100% defeat."

This response illustrates that chess is a purely logical space where both opponents engage in strategies, meaning logical schemes of reality. Introducing a random element leads to inevitable defeat. Even playing an infinite number of random games against Kasparov, one would never win, neither by mistake nor by chance. Each move must have a purpose and fit into a plan. In chess, randomness disrupts and destroys even the best plans.

What about decisions for rational managers? When tossing a coin might be an advisable strategy.

While initially alarming to introduce randomness into a rational decision-making process, as randomness is inherently defined by the absence of patterns and stands in stark contrast to what we have explored in De Groot's strategic thinking model, there are indeed several instances where randomness can be rationally justified. There even exists a specific term for this unconventional approach to decision-making: flipism. In a strictly rational setting, flipping a coin is not really suggested as a decision-making method. Instead, it's proposed to use the coin's outcome to gauge your emotional response. If the result brings relief, it may be advisable to proceed with that decision; if it causes discomfort, it may be better to reconsider. Using flipism as a method to evoke an emotional response and discern our true desires can be likened to the biblical story of King Solomon. Faced with two women claiming custody of the same child, Solomon suggested cutting the child in half, with each woman receiving an equal portion. The true mother, however, begged Solomon not to harm the child and instead urged him to give the child to the other woman, revealing her maternal instinct and love.

Returning to the concept of flipism in corporate settings, it may be advisable to flip a coin in various scenarios, such as:

1 When both outcomes are equally desirable and the decision-making team is deadlocked.
2 To ensure fairness and impartiality. A coin, recognized for its fairness and absence of bias, ensures complete objectivity in decision-making. Often referred to as a "fair" coin, it functions as an idealized random device with two equally probable states ("heads" and "tails"). This method is employed, for instance, in selecting jurors in Anglo-Saxon legal systems or assigning positions on ruling committees in Ancient Athenian democracy.
3 When the expected benefit of gathering information is outweighed by the cost of obtaining that information. This represents an extreme case of employing randomness in a very rational manner.
4 When astronauts in space need to decide trivial matters that could potentially lead to disagreements, such as determining who gets the last piece of cake. However, in these cases, the coin flip must be conducted carefully due to the absence of gravity, which could affect the fairness of the outcome.

Lastly, even in chess—often regarded as the pinnacle of rationality—there are instances where randomness proves useful. For example, the powerful AlphaZero neural network-based engine uses random moves to generate millions of games for self-training its hidden layers. Similarly, the Monte Carlo Tree Search (MCTS) algorithm generates random games to evaluate a chess position at a leaf of a decision tree.

After this brief exploration of randomness, let's return to rationality with weighted average vote and decision trees in the next two paragraphs. The rest of the chapter will examine how paradoxes and cognitive biases can disrupt rational decision-making processes, even within the realm of rationality.

Weighted average vote

The weighted average vote method is typically used in situations of certainty where the alternatives, their outcomes, and the evaluation criteria are known with precision. This approach is the gold standard for the evaluation of chess positions and involves the following steps:

1. Initially, a specific set of criteria is defined (such as safety and price for purchasing a new car), and each criterion is assigned a weight based on its importance to us.
2. Then, each option is evaluated according to the predefined criteria. This entails assigning a score to each option based on how well it meets each criterion.
3. Finally, the overall score for each option is determined by multiplying the weight assigned to each criterion by the score obtained for that criterion.

This methodology is commonly applied in marketing. For example, consider a scenario where clients need to choose a new car from several options (such as an economy car, sedan, sports car, or SUV). In this case, we can create a table with the criteria and their respective weights listed in the top rows, while the car alternatives are listed in the first column (see Figure 3.10).

Criteria and weights / *Alternatives*	Comfort 9	Performance 6	Safety 8	Cost 8	Image 3	**TOTAL**
Economy car	5	4	6	9	4	5,9
Sport car	6	9	7	4	8	6,5
Sedan	**9**	**8**	**8**	**5**	**9**	**7,6**
SUV	7	10	9	4	7	7,3

Figure 3.10 Weighted average vote

In the above example:

1 First, we assign weights to each criterion based on their importance to us. For example, we assigned a weight of 9 to comfort and 8 to both safety and cost, as these are the features we consider most crucial for our decision.
2 Second, we evaluate each option (economy, sports car, sedan, SUV) against each criterion. For instance, under the comfort criterion, the economy car is the least comfortable, receiving a score of five, while the sedan is the most comfortable, earning a score of nine.
3 Finally, we calculate the weighted average score by multiplying each evaluation by the corresponding criterion weight. In this case, the sedan emerges as the top choice with a weighted average score of 7.6.

This analytical tool is seldom used for everyday decisions (where we tend to prefer a more flexible approach), but it is highly valuable for marketing experts. It helps classify consumer behavior based on well-defined choices or consumption patterns. The tool supports not only the identification of product or service characteristics but also the planning and targeting of promotional campaigns. Additionally, these tables can serve as data for creating strategy canvases within the Blue Ocean methodology, visually illustrating the differences between various options.

A classical instance of the application of the weighted average vote in chess dates back to the early stages of AI development when Alan Turing devised the foundational chess-playing Turochamp algorithm in 1948. The algorithm, detailed in Box 3.1, adheres to the steps outlined earlier, namely:

1 Identifies seven criteria: Mobility, piece safety, King mobility and King safety, castling, pawn credit, check, and mate threats
2 Proposes an evaluation function for each criterion.
3 Weights for each criterion are embedded in the evaluation function.

Box 3.1 Turing's algorithm to play chess

1 Mobility: For the Queen, Rooks, and Bishops, add the square roots of the number of moves that the piece can make, counting a capture as two moves.
2 Piece safety: For the Rooks, Bishops, and Knights, add 1 point if there is one defender and 1.5 if there is more than one.
3 King mobility: For the King, use the same method of scoring as for the piece, but do not count castling.

4 King safety: Deduct points for the King's vulnerability, defined as the number of moves that a Queen could make was it on the square of the King.
5 Castling: Add 1 point if castling is still legally possible after this move. Add another point if castling is immediately possible or if a castling move has just been made.
6 Pawn credit: Score 2 points for each rank advanced and 3 points for each pawn defended by one or more non-pawns.
7 Check and mate threats: Score 1 point for the threat of mate and 5 points for a check; material values used for each of the pieces were: pawn = 1, Knight = 3, Bishop = 3.5, Rook = 5, Queen = 10.

Thus, the evaluation of options in both chess and marketing appears to converge through this shared methodology.

Decision trees

Decision trees are the optimal decision-making method for scenarios where agents take turns making moves in a sequential order. Decision trees feature a hierarchical tree structure consisting of a root node, branches, internal nodes, and leaf nodes. Figure 3.11 illustrates a simplified structure of a decision tree for moves in the game of chess.

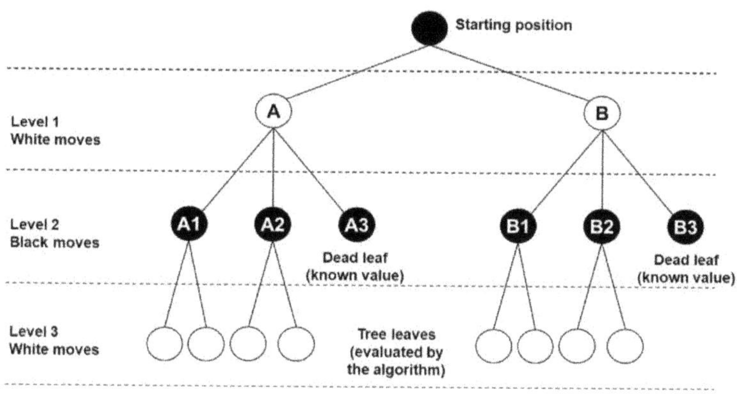

Figure 3.11 Decision tree in chess

In this example, from the starting position (root node), White has two choices (branches): moves A or B (internal nodes). In the next round, let's assume that Black has three options (A1, A2, A3) in response to White's A move, and three options (B1, B2, B3) in response to White's B move, continuing in this manner to build the branches of the decision tree with all possible alternatives. Note that positions A3 and B3 are identified as "dead leaves", characterized by a precise evaluation (checkmate, draw, known ending, etc.) that requires no further investigation.

The depth at which we decide to stop the tree (step 3 in the example) determines the "leaves" or nodes from which no further branches of analysis extend. At the level of these final leaves, an evaluation is performed using an appropriate algorithm (based on the weighted average vote, similar to what Turochamp envisaged), which assigns the leaf a numeric score. Since static evaluation functions can be unreliable, alternative methods have emerged. Particularly effective is the MCTS, a heuristic algorithm often integrated with neural networks. MCTS estimates the value of each node by simulating a number of random games starting from that node until the game reaches a conclusion (such as checkmate or a known endgame). It then selects the move that resulted in the most victories during these simulations.

In sequential games, most pre-neural network software employs the Minimax decision-making methodology. The Minimax aims for each player to minimize the maximum payoff possible for their opponent, effectively minimizing their own maximum loss in zero-sum games. In summary, the algorithm selects moves that limit the opponent's best options. The Minimax algorithm identifies the optimal move at a given node by evaluating outcomes from the bottom of the tree up to the current situation. Let's clarify with an example from the same tree diagram in the previous image.

The first step for the chess software is to assign a value to all the leaf nodes at the final level (level 3 in the chart above), as well as to any dead leaves at higher levels (level 2 in the chart above), using evaluation functions similar to the Turochamp algorithm.

Then, the Minimax algorithm operates as follows:

1 Starting at level 3, White will choose the move that maximizes its value, with these values being reported to the upper nodes.
2 At level 2, Black will select the move that minimizes White's advantage, and these values are then passed up to level 1.
3 At level 1, White will make the move that maximizes its own advantage.

This algorithm ensures that each player minimizes their potential loss in the worst-case (maximum loss) scenario.

However, to explain the Minimax algorithm, we have assumed the following mechanisms, each representing a fundamental challenge:

- Optimal stopping: At what depth does the algorithm stop analyzing the tree?
- Evaluation function: How do we assign a value to the position where we have decided to stop?
- Complexity management: How do we manage the complexity of the tree generated after only a few steps?

Regarding the first challenge, known as optimal stopping or the search for the horizon, there are several strategies available to determine the depth of analysis in the algorithm:

1 One straightforward approach is to fix a depth limit for analysis, such as stopping at the 3rd level of branching down the tree. However, this method has a drawback: it may overlook an imminent checkmate, for instance at level 4, resulting in an inaccurate evaluation of the position since it fails to anticipate the checkmate in the next move.
2 Another approach, albeit more complex, is to continue the analysis until reaching a terminal node, where the outcome is known (such as a draw, checkmate, or a known endgame). However, this method faces a significant drawback: current technology lacks the computational power to explore deeply enough in the rapidly expanding tree to reliably reach such terminal nodes.
3 A more sophisticated approach involves an algorithm known as "quiescence search" which aims to assign values only to "quiet" positions—those where there are no decisive tactical moves available. The algorithm halts when it reaches a quiet position and applies the evaluation function to assess it. Conversely, if a position is deemed unquiet or interesting, the algorithm continues expanding the branches of the tree. This mechanism reflects human intuition by avoiding to invest effort in uninteresting positions. Conversely, the algorithm focuses its exploration on positions deemed interesting—typically characterized by high piece activity or complex quantitative assessments that frequently produce divergent results when analyzed with different heuristic functions.

Applying the Minimax algorithm to complex decision trees can lead to the development of powerful simplification techniques, such as the alpha-beta pruning, which enables the algorithm to disregard entire branches that are irrelevant to the Minimax process. Let's illustrate this concept with the example as per Figure 3.12.

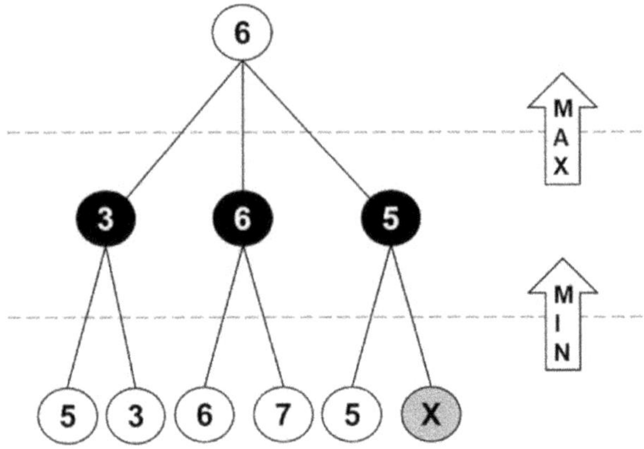

Figure 3.12 Alpha-beta pruning

Let's demonstrate that we can disregard the node marked with an X, as it cannot possibly influence the final value at the uppermost level. In fact, if X >= 5, the value in the node at the higher level remains 5, unchanged, because we will choose the minimum between the two values 5 and X; if X < 5, such as X = 2, the node at the higher level becomes 2 instead of 5. However, this change is irrelevant because, during the transition to the uppermost level, where we choose the maximum value among 3, 6, and 5 (or its substitute if X < 5), the choice will always be 6. This shows that the analysis of node X does not affect the final result.

To conclude this paragraph, we will briefly discuss decision forests, where multiple decision trees collaborate to improve prediction accuracy beyond what a single tree can achieve on its own. Decision forests find practical use in email spam detection, image classification, and medical diagnosis. However, detailed technical explanations would complicate matters and exceed the scope of this book.

Therefore, we will focus on exploring the practical applications of decision trees in situations of uncertainty, a common occurrence in business contexts.

Decision trees in situations of uncertainty

Decision trees with associated statistics are the typical decision-making methods in situations of uncertainty when the outcomes depend on the environment, which is known in a probabilistic way. In such cases, the tree is structured like a flowchart: internal nodes pose "tests" on attributes, branches reflect test outcomes, and leaf nodes denote decisions based on computed attributes. Let's illustrate this with an example.

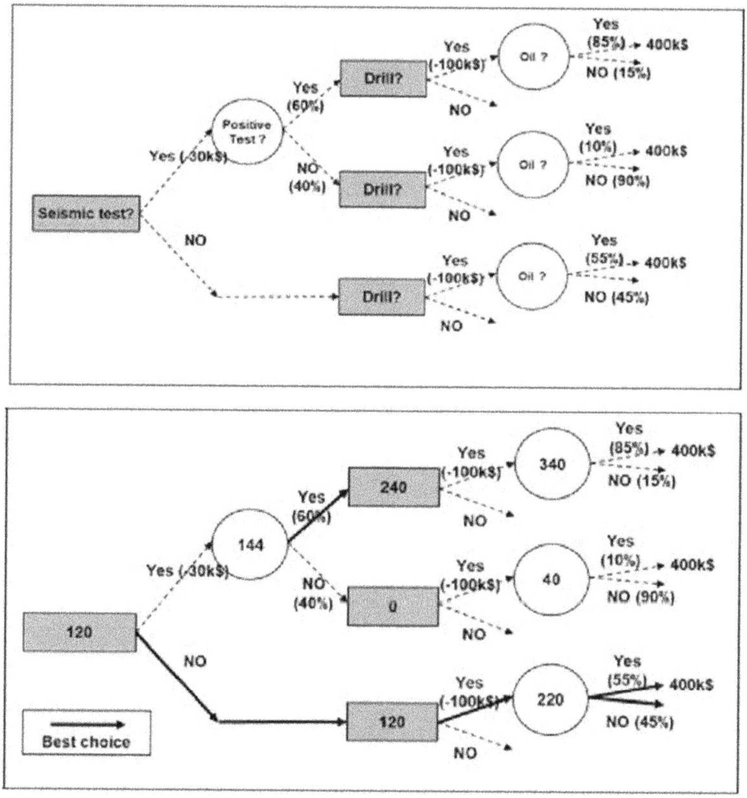

Figure 3.13 Decision tree in a management context

Let's consider a typical scenario faced by an oil company deciding whether to drill for oil. The drilling costs are $100,000, and historically, there is a 55% chance of finding oil. Alternatively, the company can conduct a seismic test before drilling, costing $30,000. Seismic tests offer more reliable insights into the likelihood of success: if the test is positive (60% probability), the chance of finding oil after drilling increases to 85%. Conversely, if the test is negative (40% probability), the chance drops to 10%. The potential gain from finding oil is $400,000. Therefore, the decision boils down to whether it is justified spending an additional $30,000 for more accurate probabilities of finding oil.

The decision-making process is illustrated in Figure 3.13 using a decision tree format. Circles represent uncontrollable events where outcomes are probabilistically known. Rectangles denote decision points where managers have control over the choices.

To determine the optimal choice, we must compute the expected values. At each circle node (representing uncontrollable events), we'll calculate the average of potential outcomes weighted by their probabilities. At each rectangle node (representing decision points), we'll assess the value of the best available option. Below are the value calculations for each option:

Then the choice is between the two options: "don't perform the seismic test" (expected value of 120k$) and "perform the test" (expected value of 144k$ minus the 30k$ for the cost of the test = 114 k$). The choice therefore falls on "drill without a seismic test".

Disruptions to the decision-making process

So far, we have explored the strategic thinking processes of chess masters and chess software, under the assumption that chess represents an ideal domain for rational decisions. However, in real life, this clear and linear chain of operations is frequently disrupted by various factors, which we will examine in the remainder of this chapter, including emotions, paradoxes, biases, and more.

Chess and the role of emotions in decision-making

Researchers frequently highlight the dominant influence of emotions over logic in decision-making. Neurologist and scientist Antonio Damasio, in his book *Descartes' Error: Emotion, Reason, and the Human Brain*[7] documented the case of Phineas Gage, who experienced brain damage in a work-related accident. This injury impaired Gage's capacity to experience emotions, which consequently affected his ability to make even simple decisions. This case underscores that decision-making processes cannot be separated from emotions.

To elucidate the distinct yet complementary roles of logic and emotions in decision-making processes, we will use a straightforward example from chess openings.

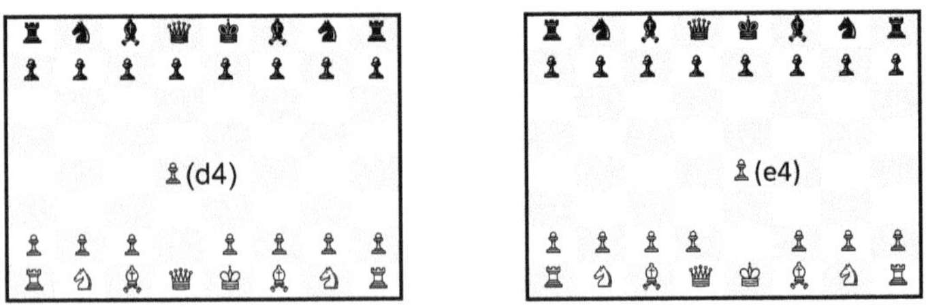

Figure 3.14 Most common opening moves in chess[8]

The two most commonly used initial moves in chess are d4 (advancing the Queen's pawn two squares forward, as shown in Figure 3.14 on the chessboard to the left) and e4 (advancing the King's pawn two squares forward, as shown in Figure 3.14 on the chessboard to the right). These moves are so popular that, among chess players, it's common to ask: "Are you an e4 or d4 type of person?" as though that move defines the player's personality.

Based on chess game statistics and analysis from chess software, both moves e4 and d4 show similar probabilities of winning or losing. Nevertheless, players consistently favor one move over the other. If the decision were purely logical, players would alternate between the two moves. However, when deciding on the first move, players associate positive or negative emotions with each option—recalling either a brilliant victory or a bitter defeat from their historical playing experience—which influences their pleasure or discomfort in choosing one over the other.

The conclusion is that when faced with two equally viable options, the final decision is usually driven by emotions. This does not negate the importance of thorough analysis; rather, it suggests that emotions should guide the final decision only after completing diligent quantitative evaluations. In the e4 versus d4 debate, emotions ultimately determine the choice of move without the fear of making a mistake, as millions of games throughout history have shown that both options are quantitatively equal.

This role of emotions as the ultimate decision-maker reflects De Groot's emphasis on the final phase of his strategic thinking process, the verification phase, where he highlighted that two conditions must be met for a decision to be made[9]:

1 One option must clearly dominate all the others quantitatively. This must be supported by thorough analysis (in the case of d4 versus e4, extensive game data provide robust statistics to justify choosing either move).
2 The qualitative argument must be subjectively convincing. This statement clearly takes into account the emotional component that each alternative evokes in the decision-maker. So, when faced with two equivalent options, this second condition ultimately determines the final decision.

This approach recognizes the importance of balancing logical analysis and emotional intuition in decision-making processes. Emotions should not prematurely influence decisions during strategic thinking. Doing so could result in suboptimal choices, potentially selecting options of lesser value based on whim. It also indicates a lack of commitment and may reflect laziness and overconfidence.

Without emotions, two perfectly equivalent options like d4 and e4 would lead us into the Buridan's ass paradox, where a donkey placed precisely midway between two stacks of hay cannot choose between them and consequently dies of hunger. This illustrates that without emotions, playing chess would be impossible because we would be incapable of deciding on the first move.

Decision-making paradoxes

Paradoxes in decision-making occur when the ultimate decision starkly contradicts previously set constraints or when a decision shifts despite no change in the underlying assumptions.

In a broader sense, paradoxes represent statements or propositions that appear absurd or contradictory. For example, "This sentence is false" and "I am lying" are two different formulations of the liar's paradox. This paradox arises because both statements result in a contradiction. For the first proposition, "This sentence is false": if it is true, then it must be false; conversely, if it is false, then it must be true. Socrates' famous quote, "I know that I know nothing", is another example of these so-called self-referential paradox.

Another famous paradox from ancient Greece is Achilles and the tortoise, first proposed by the ancient Greek philosopher Zeno of Elea. It posits that in a race where Achilles competes against a tortoise over a distance of 10 meters and the tortoise is given a 1-meter head start, Achilles will never overtake the tortoise. Zeno argues that Achilles must first reach the point where the tortoise began, but by the time he gets there, the tortoise will have moved forward slightly. Achilles must then reach the new position of the tortoise, and this process continues infinitely. As a result, Zeno concludes that Achilles will never catch up to the tortoise. A similar paradox is the arrow paradox, also known as the impossibility of motion. If an arrow is shot toward a target, it must first travel halfway to the target. Before reaching halfway, it must cover a quarter of the distance. Before traveling a quarter of the way, it must travel one-eighth, and before an eighth, one-sixteenth, and so forth. This infinite division suggests that the arrow never actually moves, implying that motion is merely an illusion.

Throughout history, paradoxes have been a powerful catalyst for advances in logic and philosophy. Let's now explore some of the paradoxes in decision-making.

The decision on the decision method to make the decision

The first paradox in decision-making theory pertains to the decision-making process itself where the initial step is determining the appropriate decision-making method to use.

In a sense, this falls into the category of self-referential paradoxes: to make a decision, I first need to decide how to decide.

Formally, the paradox arises from the observation that, in several situations, different decision-making methods produce different results with the same dataset. A typical business scenario is when a CFO is invited to present various investment options to the Board of Directors. Before delving into the financial details, the CFO emphasizes the importance of selecting the criteria for evaluating these investments. However, because the CFO understands precisely how the criteria will affect each investment option, influencing the Board's choice of criteria indirectly shapes the decision on which investment to pursue. Therefore, it's crucial to be cautious in situations where you are asked to choose decision criteria. Always insist on understanding how these criteria impact each option before making a decision.

The choice of wine at the restaurant

We'll illustrate this second decision-making paradox with an example from everyday life.

Imagine you are a college student with a limited budget, and the girl you've liked for a long time has finally accepted your invitation. You decide on a fancy restaurant for your first date. After ordering your courses, the waiter asks you to choose the wine. You see two categories: expensive wines and cheap wines. Considering your budget, you avoid the most expensive category. You also steer clear of the cheapest wines to avoid appearing overly thrifty. Instead, you're likely to choose something near the top of the range in the cheap category, balancing both your budget limitations and your desire to make a favorable impression.

However, if the menu had a third category for champagne and very expensive wines, your decision-making process would likely change, possibly leading you to choose something in the middle of the expensive category.

In more technical terms, this situation illustrates the ranking reversal paradox: without changing the ranking of the options or your available budget, the addition of a third category alters your choice. This paradox highlights how the introduction of a new option can shift decisions, even though a rational agent would be expected to make the same choices under consistent conditions.

The St. Petersburg paradox

Decision trees are powerful and effective tools for organizing and managing highly complex problems. However, they are unfortunately plagued by a paradox.

Let's consider a scenario where we participate in a bet, such as choosing red (R) or black (B) on a roulette wheel.

So you walk into a casino and decide to employ the following strategy: Each time you place a bet and you lose, you should repeat the same bet but with double the money.

Here's how it works:

You start by betting $1 on red:

- If red comes up, you win $1.
- If black comes up, you lose your $1. Next, you double your bet for the next round, so you bet $2 on red.
    - If red comes up, you win $2 minus the $1 you lost at the previous round = you gain $1 .
    - If black comes up, you lose your $2. Next, you double your bet again, so you bet $4 on red:
        - If red comes up, you win $4 minus 2$ and 1$ you lost in the previous rounds = you gain $1.
        - If black comes up, you lose your $4. Next, you double your bet again, so you bet $8 on red.

It can be demonstrated mathematically that each time red comes up, you gain $1, no matter how late it comes up in a sequence (see Figure 3.15). If you continue playing this strategy for N rounds, you will accumulate N dollars, with N being as large as you wish.

So, theoretically, you could bankrupt the casino and become a millionaire.

Would you consider using this approach at the roulette table during your next visit to a casino?

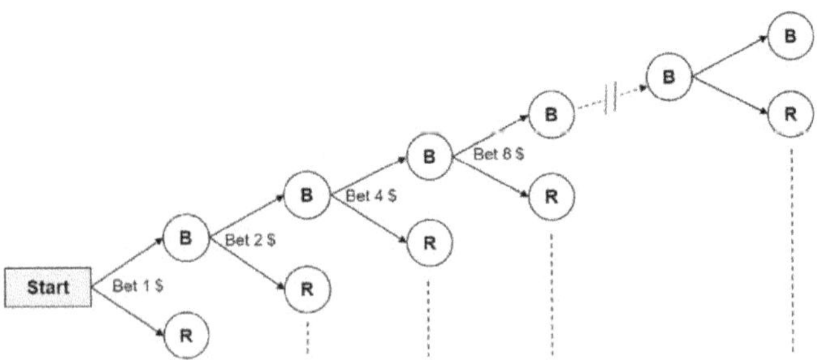

Gain if Red comes out	1$	2$	4$	8$	$2^k \$$
Cumulative loss in previous rounds	0$	1$	3$ (=1+2)	7$ (=1+2+4)	$2^k\text{-}1\$=1+2+...+2^{k-1}$
Net gain	1$	1$	1$	1$	1$

Figure 3.15 The St. Petersburg paradox

You feel a strong temptation, but since this strategy falls within the paradoxes of decision-making, your intuition warns you that something may not be quite right.

In fact, it can be mathematically demonstrated that this strategy, rather than ensuring a gain of N dollars (where N can be as large as desired), will inevitably result in losing all the dollars you bring into the casino.

Without entering the technical details, we can say that there will be a long series of losing bets such that doubling your stakes becomes impossible. This occurs because you will have exhausted all the money you initially brought to the casino, as well as any gains from earlier rounds. Note that doubling means that after a streak of 20 losing bets you will need to bet 2^{20} totaling over $100,000.Therefore, not being able to double the stake at some point, you have no possibility to recover the losses at the following round. You will have lost everything.

This demonstrates the power of exponential growth, reminiscent of the legend of grains on a chessboard. According to an ancient tale, the King of India, seeking entertainment, promised a reward to anyone who could amuse him. A mathematician invented the game of chess and captivated the King with it. When asked about his desired reward, the mathematician declined gold or money. Instead, he requested a single grain of wheat on the first square of the chessboard, two grains on the second square, and continued doubling the amount for each subsequent square.

Initially, the King and his court found the request trivial and amusing. However, the King agreed, instructing his vizier to fulfill the mathematician's wishes. Much to everyone's astonishment, the vizier later returned to inform the King that the mathematician's request had exhausted all the wheat in the entire empire.

Decision-making biases

While paradoxes are intellectually stimulating, they are rare in real-life decisions. More commonly—indeed, endemic—are cognitive biases that influence decision-making.

Women say 80% of men are "below average", while 80% of men think they are "above average".[10]

This is an entertaining illustration of the attribution bias, which suggests that we often attribute our successes to our own skills and abilities while blaming external factors for our failures. Conversely, we tend to attribute other people's successes to luck, and their failures to their own mistakes.

Generally speaking, decision biases refer to systematic deviations from rational decision-making processes, often influenced by cognitive or emotional factors, which can result into suboptimal choices.

Cognitive biases are often essential in decision-making, particularly when an overload of information would overwhelm our cognitive capacities. If the root cause of cognitive biases is the challenge of processing excessive information, how does this apply to AI, which possesses nearly unlimited computational and analytical power?

Despite the objective nature of computer analyses and its nearly unlimited computational power, AI still suffers from cognitive biases. This is because the training of neural networks involves feeding the system with human-produced content, which inherently includes human biases.

What about chess and cognitive biases? In this context, the situation becomes more intriguing.

Chess is often considered an ideal domain where biases are absent, as the game's outcome provides an objective evaluation of the decisions made during play. However, human chess players are still susceptible to biases, and we will compare these biases with those of managers at the end of this paragraph.

However, chess players, much like managers, are susceptible to falling into the allure of cognitive biases, which are so varied and compelling that resisting them can seem nearly impossible.

The situation changes drastically when considering AI and chess. Unlike other AI activities such as image, speech, and text recognition, the training of neural networks in chess does not involve any human evaluation. The only criterion for the output layer is victory or loss, providing a truly objective evaluation metric.

By the way, I asked ChatGPT, "What percentage of men are below average?" The answer was approximately 50%. It seems that even AI aims to avoid displeasing either men or women by using the word "approximately" to allow some flexibility in interpretation.

Here is a compilation of key biases that affect both chess players and managers alike:

Sunk cost fallacy: This bias involves persisting with a course of action due to prior investments (such as time, money, or effort) rather than objectively reassessing the current situation. In chess, players may press on with an attack even when it becomes clear it won't achieve the anticipated results, simply because they've committed many pieces to it. Similarly, managers may continue with an investment strategy despite diminishing returns, justifying it by the substantial resources already allocated. This is notably evident in large-scale projects like infrastructure or extensive marketing campaigns. The common rationale for continuation is often framed as: "We can't abandon the effort now after investing so much".

Selective search for evidence or selective perception is a bias that occurs commonly among both managers and chess players. They tend to seek out facts and evidence that confirm a particular conclusion while disregarding or downplaying other facts that might support a different conclusion. This selective approach to data and events can lead to dismissing information that does not align with preconceived notions or early-stage decisions. This bias often arises when decisions are made prematurely in the strategic planning process, before thorough analysis is complete, which necessitates justifying hasty and impulsive decisions through a selective search for evidence.

Mental inertia is a bias marked by a reluctance to alter established thought patterns, even when new circumstances demand a fresh approach. We've observed that the process of strategic thinking, necessary for making optimal decisions, can consume considerable mental energy. When our mental resources are depleted, decisions tend to prioritize conserving energy. This is when mental inertia often takes hold, leaning on past experiences rather than adapting to new situations.

Anchoring is a well-known bias in business negotiations where the initial quantitative information significantly influences the course of the negotiating process by setting a reference point for subsequent dynamics. Initially theorized by Kahneman,[11] this bias was demonstrated through studies where participants estimated the percentage of African nations in the UN. Those asked if the percentage was "more or less than 10%" tended to give lower estimates (averaging 25%), while those asked if it was "more or less than 65%" gave higher estimates (averaging 45%). In chess, this bias appears more subtly. For example, a player who chooses an aggressive and tactical opening may maintain an aggressive mindset throughout the game, even if the position later evolves into a simplified and balanced endgame.

The observed and classified biases are more than 150, all of which are very frequent in the decision-making processes. As it is not the objective of this chapter to discuss such a vast repertoire, for those interested in an in-depth analysis, there are dedicated publications available for further reading.

To decide or not to decide: that is the question

We normally assume that being in a position to make a decision is always beneficial, as good decisions are expected to improve our situation.

However, there are scenarios where decision-makers are at a disadvantage simply because they are required to make a decision.

In chess, such situations are known as Zugzwang (meaning "obligation to move" in German), where any legal move will worsen the player's position, and they would be better off if they could avoid making a move altogether. In chess, Zugzwang is quite common in endings involving Kings and pawns.

A rare and sophisticated occurrence of Zugzwang in the middlegame can be found in "The Immortal Zugzwang Game", played between Friedrich Sämisch and Aron Nimzowitsch in Copenhagen in March 1923. The Zugzwang position for White was reached after Black's exceptional waiting move h6!!,[12] where any move by White would lead to defeat. If White could refrain from moving, they would be just fine.

Since understanding Zugzwang in chess requires advanced knowledge of the game, we'll explain the concept using a more familiar scenario: slicing a cake.

We all remember when we were kids and our mother used a clever strategy to avoid conflicts between siblings when sharing a slice of cake. One sibling would be tasked with slicing the cake into two parts, while the other would get to choose their piece first. This approach ensured an optimal and fair division of the cake, resulting in no complaints.

Let's make this strategy a bit more complex. Imagine that two siblings, A and B, must share a cake according to these rules: A chooses the first slice, and B cuts the cake. B must cut the cake into any number of triangular radial slices, which don't all need to be the same size. A can pick any first slice, then B and A take turns choosing a slice, always selecting one of the two slices that borders the open part of the cake. Both A and B aim to get as much of the cake as possible.

Now the question is: How can B cut the cake so that after all the slices are taken, B ends up with more cake than A? The answer involves putting A in a situation of Zugzwang. You can try to figure out the best slicing strategy for B on your own, or you can look at Figure 3.16 for a possible solution with 15 slices, which guarantees B 5/9 of the cake when L = 2*m. With such a pizza, B will get either two extra-large L slices and one m slice or one L and three m slices, depending on what A does on turn 3

Who really decides?

Okay, now it's time to sit down, relax, take a deep breath, and brace yourself for the final revelation that will challenge your deeply held beliefs about free will.

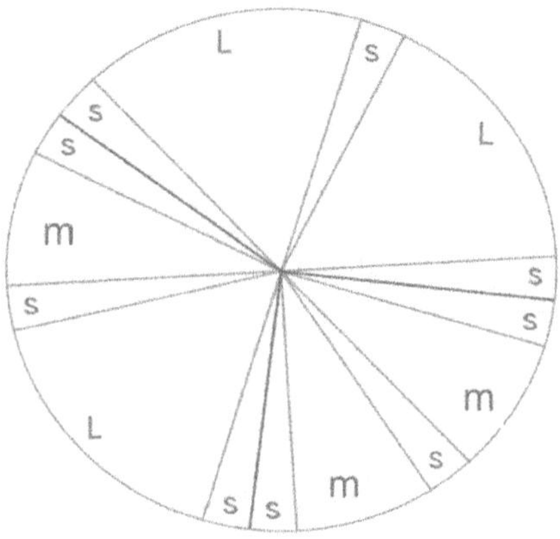

Figure 3.16 Cake slicing strategy

According to recent research by physiologist Benjamin Libet[13] on the relationship between brain activity and voluntary decisions, it appears that we, as sentient beings, might be excluded from the decision-making process we have analyzed so far. For example, if we decide to move an arm, the arm moves first, and about half a second later, our consciousness becomes aware of the decision to move the arm. Consequently, anyone monitoring our brain through a scanning system could predict our decision about half a second before we become aware of it, as the action precedes our awareness of the action. These experiments led to the perplexing conclusion that unconscious brain processes initiate actions before we become consciously aware of our decision to act, raising questions about the extent to which free will governs our actions.

While these insights might not diminish the satisfaction you derive from past good decisions, they certainly provide a convenient alibi for any wrong decisions you may make in the future.

Chapter 3—Decision-making—interviews

Luca Desiata interviewed by Bachar Kouatly

What is the most dangerous cognitive bias you have encountered during your professional life?

Well, I'm going to say something quite controversial. I am going to speak about a form of wishful thinking—the bias that leads people to believe what they want to be true, regardless of the evidence. I'm referring to Diversity and Inclusion (D&I) policies, which are commendable in themselves. However, top managers often believe that simply having their Boards approve a D&I policy and promoting it through an extensive internal communication campaign will instantly eradicate discrimination. This belief is so entrenched that companies with the strongest diversity policies tend to lower their guard, allowing homophobes, chauvinists, and racists to flourish. Warning: just as discriminatory companies will never succeed in eradicating homosexuality, which is a part of human nature, inclusive companies will never succeed in eradicating homophobia, which is also part of human nature.

What about paradoxes?

I have a funny story about the Saint Petersburg paradox. Although I'm convinced this method wouldn't work to become a millionaire, my conviction faltered when one of the students in my Chess and Corporate Strategy Course at Luiss Business School mentioned that he had tried it in a casino and was promptly escorted out by security. In class, we all thought that if casino security intervened to stop someone from using the Saint Petersburg routine, there must be something to fear in that method. After all, casinos are considered bastions of rationality applied to statistics.

Some funny story about decision-making methods?

A student in my Chess and Corporate Strategy Course at Luiss Business School once asked if the 37% rule from the Dowry dilemma could also apply to finding the true love of our lives. Later, I came across some interesting statistics indicating that the average European has around ten partners throughout their lifetime. This translates into "using" the first three or four partners to set standards and then selecting the first partner who surpasses those initial experiences as the one for life. After all, who would want to settle down with their high school crush, fearing they might miss out on what else the world has to offer? Thus, a certain degree of experimentation can help establish the minimum standard for the love life we aspire to have.

Do you have any other interesting episode related to the decision-making methodologies illustrated in this chapter?

Interestingly enough, I vividly recall two practical instances of employing the flipism methodology. During my tenure as CEO of the Italian State company Sogin, two of my Executive Vice Presidents approached me to determine who should take responsibility for Institutional Affairs. Personally, I considered it essential to have that role filled and trusted both managers equally, making the decision indifferent to me. However, I wanted to avoid causing resentment by choosing one over the other. Therefore, recognizing the advantage of avoiding personal conflicts when faced with equally viable options, I resorted to flipism. I flipped a coin in the presence of the two candidates and made my decision based on the outcome.

The situation took an amusing turn afterward. For such first line appointments, my decision typically required approval from the Board of Directors. To my discomfort, during the board meeting, neither candidate seemed to secure a majority of votes. I feared I might need to resort to flipism a second time for the same decision, which would have been unprecedented in the annals of decision-making. Fortunately, the Chairman of the Board, who held a casting vote worth two votes, broke the deadlock and affirmed my—or rather, the coin's—decision.

The second occasion also relates to my term as CEO of the Italian State company Sogin. Seeking to enhance fairness in the public procurement process and mitigate potential external influences, I explored with my procurement EVP the concept of employing flipism to select the winning supplier from a pool of technically qualified applicants. To our surprise, we learned that the Italian authority overseeing public procurement had contemplated the use of flipism to bolster the resilience of the procurement process. We engaged with them and offered to conduct some trials, but this initiative never materialized due to logistical challenges.

Are you more of an e4 or d4 chess player? And what's the reason behind your preference?

I am definitely an e4 player; I don't think I've ever played d4 in my entire life. The reason for this preference is hard to pinpoint. It likely stems from the first chess book I studied, which I found in the local public library of the small town where I grew up. This 19th-century publication predates many of the theoretical developments of the 20th century, so I shaped my chess style around romantic openings like the King's Gambit and the Evans Gambit, both starting with e4. I still remember the book classifying the Sicilian Defense as inferior for Black, so I never bothered to learn how to counter it. Being my first chess book, it had an imprinting effect on me, almost like a biblical revelation, and I never questioned its contents. Only after repeatedly losing to the Sicilian Defense, did I realize that the book's judgment on this opening was outdated.

In my opinion, this episode demonstrates how non-dogmatic the world of chess is. There is no absolute authority; only the harsh reality of game results matters.

To what extent has AI technology contributed to this publication?

I conceived the concept and content of Chess and Corporate Strategy in 2012, a time when practical AI writing tools were non-existent.

As a non-native English speaker, I must acknowledge that I relied extensively on AI for style review in creating this English version.

I was impressed by the AI's ability to understand the meaning of sentences and improve their style and clarity. However, I was deeply disappointed when I asked it to create additional content for some chapters of the book. What it produced was rather dull and schematic.

What do you think about Libet's experiments?

This is the finding I struggle with the most. For managers, chess players, and indeed every human being, it's incredibly difficult to accept that we might not be in control of our own conscious decisions. Nonetheless, science is science, and we can't just dismiss results we find uncomfortable. Fortunately, I discovered that Libet himself tried to reinterpret his experiments by introducing electrical potential into the brain to uphold the idea of free will.

Anatoly Karpov interviewed by Bachar Kouatly

Can chess players be considered perfect human decision-making machines?

Chess players certainly cannot be considered perfect decision-making machines. This is evident from the simple fact that most chess games are won or lost due to mistakes made by both players. The winner is typically the one who makes the second-to-last mistake. Mistakes often arise from erroneous calculations, but more frequently, they result from flaws in the strategic decision-making process. Below are some considerations on some of the most common decision-making biases in chess practice.

Attributive asymmetry

If I win, I'll likely attribute the victory to my skill in inducing my opponent to make a mistake rather than to my opponent's error. If I lose, I'll tend to blame external factors unrelated to my abilities, such as fatigue or adverse circumstances. Regardless of how we interpret these situations, one principle holds true in chess: you either win or lose, and there are no excuses. A piece on the chessboard cannot move by itself.

When you win, many friends will join in the celebrations.

When you lose, you lose alone!

Anchoring

Anchoring in chess rarely occurs due to a quantitative evaluation of a particular move, sequence, or variation. More often, chess players become fixated on a specific interpretation of the position. When this happens, they find it difficult to shift their perspective to adapt to the actual situation. If our opponent notices that we are trapped in this cognitive bias that hampers our evaluative ability, they can exploit the flaws in our reasoning. Anchoring in chess is tied to ideas and patterns, not numerical values. Generally, this will lead to inevitable defeat.

A common scenario is when we find ourselves in an inferior position and set a draw as our best possible outcome. Even if the position suddenly shifts in our favor, we remain anchored to the original goal of a draw and fail to seize the unexpected opportunity to win.

Another example is when we realize we've blundered. Few people will admit the mistake and try to return to the initial position, which usually just wastes time. Instead, we want to prove to ourselves and our opponent that the move made sense and wasn't a blunder. By doing so, we display consistency but end up digging our own grave. This justifies the popular saying, "Mistakes come in pairs" or "Mistakes never happen alone".

Peer pressure

A beginner falls prey to this type of decision bias due to their limited understanding of positional elements. A champion, however, does not feel pressured when others have different opinions. Their mind must be free to constantly question everything, even against the computer or their team's assessments. I believe the quality of play and depth of understanding among today's champions, such as Anand, is quite shallow due to their excessive reliance on computer analysis and judgment. In this case, peer pressure becomes software pressure.

Selective search of evidence

Selective search for evidence in chess happens when we oversimplify the complexity of a position to stay within our comfort zone. A true champion constantly challenges "evidence", even if it comes from computers. A champion must remain a moving target; as soon as they stop moving and declare something as "evident", they are lost.

Mental inertia
This category encompasses the previous two cases: peer pressure and selective search for evidence. Inertia occurs when we prefer to listen to others' opinions or have already decided on a move. This observation—that mental inertia results from two other biases—suggests that chess can serve as a valuable testing ground to explore the correlations between various decision-making biases. Currently, there is no unified theory to interpret these biases. Following the experiments by De Groot and Chase & Simon, decision biases could be the next area of research application for chess.

Conforming to the role
"Conforming to the role" is a common phenomenon observed during world championships on both sides of the chessboard. The reigning champion, fearful of losing the title, will tend to play cautiously, while the challenger will generally adopt a more aggressive and determined approach.

I was largely immune to this bias. I believe my approach remained consistent throughout my chess career, whether as the reigning champion or as the challenger. I played every tournament, world championship, and simultaneous game, whether against beginners or masters, without seeking shortcuts. My ultimate goal has always been the pursuit of balanced positions, consistency, and perfection.

Fatigue
Fatigue is the primary cause of errors in chess. Every move requires a significant amount of energy and making decisions in a prolonged game or tournament demands excellent physical and mental condition. Resilience, a predisposition for continuous decision-making, strong health, good habits, and excellent stress-management skills are essential for a successful champion. For me, sleep, walking, swimming, and tennis are key factors in managing stress. In high-level tournaments, the first signs of sleep-wake cycle disruption usually appear around the 15th game. During our long matches in the '80s and '90s, I'm sure Kasparov experienced similar sleep disturbances, even though he was ten years younger than me. My personal method to counter this is to wake up naturally in the morning, ensuring I have fully recovered my energy. Sleep is crucial for any professional activity requiring strategic thinking, as it helps us reorganize ideas, plans, and solutions to problems—a kind of extended "transitional" phase, as described in De Groot's studies.

Fatigue in decision-making processes can also be exploited to our advantage. By diverting our opponent's energy toward secondary objectives, we can make them tired and vulnerable when it's time to focus on the critical issues that determine the outcome of the game.

Notes

1 https://hbr.org/2010/06/the-decision-driven-organization.
2 M. A. Nielsen. *Neural Networks and Deep Learning* (Determination Press, 2015).
3 C. Shannon. Programming a Computer for Playing Chess, 1950, London UK.
4 S. Zweig. *The Royal Game: A Chess Story* (Pushkin Press, November 4, 2021) London, UK.
5 H. P. Moravec, *Mind Children: The Future of Robot and Human Intelligence* (Cambridge: Harvard University Press, 1988).
6 https://it.hobby.scacchi.narkive.com/82x83jCj/kasparov-e-la-strategia.
7 A. Damasio. *Descartes' Error: Emotion, Reason, and the Human Brain* (Grosset/Putnam, 1994).
8 Chessboards drawn using Unicode chess pieces by piliapp.com
9 A. De Groot. *Thought and Choice in Chess.* (Amsterdam University Press, 2008) (reprint).
10 https://medium.com/hello-love/women-say-80-of-men-are-below-average-bab0b8af2606.
11 A. Tversky. Daniel Kahneman. Judgment under Uncertainty: Heuristics and Biases. *Science*, New Series, Vol. 185 (1974), pp. 1–10.
12 In chess notation, a double exclamation mark signifies an exceptionally good move that is difficult to spot.
13 B. Libet. Unconscious Cerebral Initiative and the Role of Conscious Will in Voluntary Action. *Behavioral and Brain Sciences,* Vol. 8 (1985), pp. 529–566.

Chapter 4

Strategic planning

So, after an exhausting process of strategic thinking that has squeezed our brain neurons and released significant amounts of adrenaline into our bodies, we finally arrive at a strategic objective with a plan to achieve it. What do we do now?

After completing the mind journey, it's time to return to the external world and impose our intended plan onto reality.

Strategic planning is not merely an intellectual exercise for abstract enjoyment. Similar to chess, business requires decisive, warfare-like actions to achieve its objectives.

Business and the military approach

It is true that, in recent years, the business world has adopted a widespread approach of "fair play" or gentlemen's agreements. Every negotiation is expected to be win-win, every marketing action aims to expand the market, benefiting competitors as well. The zero-sum concept seems to have disappeared from business language and practice.

However, every manager knows from personal experience that the true nature of business is a fight to the last drop of blood, concealed behind the facade of "fair play". Business is a war where competitors are enemies to be vanquished. The manager is always on the front lines, with the ultimate goal of achieving victory in the battle for market share. With this approach in mind, scholars in the 1980s began to recognize the value of ancient military strategy knowledge and its potential application to strategic planning. Works like Sun Tzu's "The Art of War", Clausewitz's "On War", and Mao Zedong's "Little Red Book" quickly became business classics, inspiring marketing theorists.

In the military approach to strategic marketing, two primary war strategies can be identified: offensive and defensive. Each has several variations, which we will analyze in this chapter.

The traditional view of business as intense competition originates from Harvard Professor Michael Porter, who introduced his Five Forces

DOI: 10.4324/9781003533719-4

Framework in the Harvard Business Review in 1979.[1] This model supports the notion that business competition is fundamentally a battle among rivals.

Let's see how fighting along each of Porter's forces[2] can enhance the company's value.

- Fighting to master the first force "customer bargaining power" would enhance our ability to set higher prices for our products and services; let's call this unit sale price P_u.
- Fighting to master the second force "supplier bargaining power" would enhance our ability to lower the cost for our products and services; let's call this unit production cost C_u.
- Fighting to master the third and fourth forces, "the threat of new entrants to the industry" and "the ability of customers to find substitutes for the sector's products" would enhance our ability to maximize the quantity of products sold; let's call this quantity Q.

Therefore, fighting on the market along these four dimensions will enable the company to maximize its value V. In fact if we consider the following simplified formula for the valuation of the company:

V = M x EBITDA, where V is the company value, M is the sector specific valuation multiple, and EBITDA is the total margin, approximately given by:

$$EBITDA = Q \times (P_u - C_u)$$

It is evident that mastering the forces in Porter's market model will directly enhance each component of the EBITDA formula, thereby boosting the overall company valuation. Therefore, fighting and winning the competition war means increasing the company's value in competitive markets.

This clearly demonstrates the warfare-like nature of business, linking the dimensions of the fight to the value components.

Chess and war

"Chess! What is it good for? War, of course". So begins an article in The Guardian in 2004.[3]

Additionally, the former world champion Bobby Fischer famously said, "Chess is a war over the board. The objective is to crush the opponent's mind".

Everything in chess echoes war: the military terminology, the types of pieces, the chessboard configuration with two opposing armies, and the objective of annihilating the adversary. The game of chess spread across continents alongside armies, absorbing military traditions.

The origins of chess can be traced back to certain military legends. According to some sources, it was invented in the 12th century BC during the siege of Troy by Palamedes, a Greek commander, to illustrate army deployment in battles. More reliable sources, however, trace the origins of chess to the 6th century AD in India under the Gupta dynasty, where it was known as Chaturanga which referred to the four divisions of the Indian army: soldiers, knights, chariots, and elephants. Chaturanga is regarded as the ancestor of chess because of two specific features: (1) pieces with distinct identities and movements, (2) the outcome depending on the fate of a single piece, the King.

As chess spread from India to Europe, it became known as Shatranj, derived from the Persian word "Shah" meaning supreme authority. The elephant piece was replaced by the less exotic minister or grand vizier. In the Islamic world, despite the religious prohibition of playing games, chess was exempt due to its military nature. According to legend, when a believer asked Caliph Omar, the Prophet Muhammad's father-in-law, why chess had not been prohibited like all other games, he responded, "Why should it be banned? It's merely a form of war".

The game spread across Europe during the 10th century with Arab expansion. Its modern form developed in medieval Europe, where monarchies were common. The term "pawn" comes from Medieval Latin, meaning "foot soldier". The Knight pieces symbolize the warriors of feudal times. The Italian "Alfiere" (standard-bearing soldier) evolved into the Bishop in England and the "fou" in France. The Rooks represented the defensive and observational towers typical of medieval landscapes.

However, the Queen has the most intriguing history of all the chess pieces. Originally a weak piece that could only move one step diagonally, it evolved into the most powerful piece by the 15th century, influenced by the prestige of Queen Isabella of Castile. Her accomplishments, such as expelling the Moors from Spain and sponsoring Christopher Columbus, played a significant role in the transformation of the Queen piece. Other influential and charismatic queens of that time, including Catherine of Aragon, Elizabeth I, Mary Stuart, and Catherine de Medici, further contributed to this evolution.

During the Age of Enlightenment, the diminishing influence of Kings and Queens was well represented in an anecdote attributed to Benjamin Franklin. In a chess game on the eve of the American War of Independence, Franklin found his King in check. Instead of moving it, he moved another piece illegally, stating, "If it were a good King, it would deserve the protection of his subjects. But ours is a tyrant and costs more than he's worth. Take it if you wish; I'll continue the battle as a Republican". This declaration embodied the revolutionary democratic spirit, eventually leading American chessboards to replace the King with a president.

In 1800, Napoleon, despite not being an exceptional chess player, asserted that he had employed new attack strategies in his military campaigns inspired by chess positions.

A century later, the Nazis adopted chess as a symbol of war, heroism, discipline, and Aryan purity, renaming it Tak-Tik and replacing traditional pieces with symbols reflecting World War II, such as aviators, soldiers, and bombs.

Recently, experts from the Organization of Science and Technology within the Australian Department of Defense have utilized advancements in chess software for military simulations. They explored various scenarios, such as analyzing dynamics where a player holds a material advantage but faces an opponent capable of making two consecutive moves, or situations involving armies with pieces invisible to the enemy, like planes evading radar detection. Given that such military strategies cannot be practically tested with real armies, chess has proven to be an ideal simulation platform for gaining insights into real-world battle scenarios. Similarly, in Sweden, analogous experiments were conducted using human players instead of computers, employing opaque plates over the chessboard to simulate limited visibility of the opponent's maneuvers.

Chess has recently been integrated into US military training for Marines to foster a more strategic and analytical thinking environment. Specifically, the US Marine Corps Infantry School-West at Camp Pendleton, California, has incorporated the game into its new 14-week training course. Marine Capt. David DeLong, Instructor Company Commander for Infantry Training Battalion-West, commented, "Chess provides us with a framework to apply tactical thinking, where we strategize using various weapon systems against a thinking enemy, similar to maneuvering chess pieces".[4]

Warfare strategies

Once the parallel with military strategy has been established, we can now draw examples from chess and military to illustrate how resource allocation is intertwined with strategic planning and overall strategy.

Offensive strategies

The impetuous nature of the struggle for market dominance is well exemplified by offensive strategies. To avoid wasting resources, an attack should focus on one target at a time, on the narrowest possible front, and only when a weakness in the opponent's deployment is identified. The attacker's advantage lies in the ability to concentrate forces on a single target, while the defender must organize their defense across the entire front.

There are several types of offensive strategies: frontal attacks, encirclement, flanking attacks, and guerrilla.

Frontal attacks

The frontal attack is a direct, face-to-face assault that typically requires deploying all available resources, including significant financial investment. In the business realm, every part of the organization—from marketing to production—must be strengthened in preparation for the assault. This strategy involves intense advertising efforts and often the development and launch of a new product.

In practice, frontal attacks are rare for two main reasons. First, they are costly: many valuable resources are lost in the assault. Second, they often fail. If the defender can reorganize their resources in time, they can nullify the attacker's strategic advantage and launch a counterattack. For instance, during World War II in 1943, the Battle of Stalingrad saw the German frontal attack on the city of Stalingrad repelled by the Soviets. This was achieved through Operation Uranus, which encircled and defeated the German Army.

The frontal attack strategy is advisable under the following conditions:

- The market is relatively homogeneous and products are scarcely differentiated
- Brand equity and customer loyalty are low
- The attacker has significantly more resources than the opponent

Before launching an offensive, it is essential to assess the opponent's strength, the time needed for them to realign resources, and the support they can gather from allies. The attack should be swift, as the element of surprise is more valuable than a thousand tanks!

Probably the most renowned frontal attack in history is the Allied invasion of Normandy in 1944 (Operation Overlord or D-Day), which succeeded in establishing a foothold on the coast thanks to its massive deployment of resources.

Frontal attacks were the standard approach in Romantic-era chess. In the 19th century, European culture was steeped in ideals of heroism, sacrifice, and idealism, which permeated every aspect of life, including chess. The best games went down in history with names like "Evergreen" or "Immortal". The Romantic player avoided sound strategic considerations and constantly sought the unexpected and brilliant sacrifice, the sublime and clever combination that would earn the audience's admiration. This passion for tactics and extravagant combinations often led to playing inferior and highly unbalanced variations, simply for the pleasure of finishing the game in a spectacular manner.

Romantic players would launch their pieces against the opponent's king's fortress, often sacrificing frontline forces in the attempt to secure victory with the relentless advance of the rear-line army. In the heat of battle, material balance was a secondary concern. What mattered most was the supreme idea of the attack, which had to prevail over everything else. The resulting games were highly spectacular and entertaining but ultimately lacking in strategic precision.

In the business world, frontal attacks are often highly visible due to significant advertising expenditure. A classic example is the everlasting rivalry between Pepsi and Coca-Cola, where both companies engage in price wars and aggressive marketing campaigns.

Encirclement

A second offensive strategy is encirclement, which is more agile and diversified than frontal attacks. Encirclement in a market can be achieved by introducing a range of products similar to those of the competitor we wish to target. Each product captures a portion of the competitor's market share, leaving them weakened, demoralized, and in a state of siege. If executed stealthily, direct confrontation can be avoided. Alternatively, encirclement can focus on market niches rather than products. The attacker expands into market niches adjacent to those of the competitor to gradually undermine them.

The encirclement strategy is recommended when the following conditions are met:

- The market is weakly segmented with some segments relatively free of strong competitors
- The attacker has strong product development resources and sufficient resources to operate in multiple segments simultaneously

In the business world, a classic example of an encirclement strategy is Google's approach to dominating the Internet landscape. Initially emerging from the search engine and online advertising businesses, Google expanded over time by launching a variety of services targeting multiple market segments simultaneously. These include email services with Gmail, online video with YouTube, web browsers with Chrome, mobile operating systems with Android, cloud services with Google Cloud, and AI with Gemini.

In the military domain, the encirclement strategy was frequently employed by the Roman Empire's army. This often led to prolonged sieges of enemy cities, such as the siege of Alesia by Julius Caesar against the Gauls led by Vercingetorix, or the siege of Carthage at the end of the third Punic War. A significant battle that led to a devastating encirclement and defeat for the Roman army was the Battle of Cannae during the second

Punic War. In this occasion, the Carthaginian forces led by Hannibal surrounded and annihilated the larger Roman army using the legendary pincer maneuver, which has since become synonymous with the encirclement strategy.

A more recent example from the beginning of WW2 is the German encirclement of the entire Maginot Line, a complex and integrated system of fortifications constructed between 1928 and 1940 by the French government to protect its eastern borders from German attacks. The fortifications were made entirely of concrete, connected by underground passages, and equipped with machine gun bunkers. The system was fortified with two layers of barbed wire and anti-tank rails, along with road and rail networks for supply lines, and concealed turrets that could emerge when needed. This impressive defense system, which cost three billion francs at the time, was based on a positional defense strategy typical of World War I. Unfortunately, it failed to account for the increased mobility of modern armies and advancements in military technology. The German invasion plan in 1940, often referred to as the "Sichelschnitt" or "sickle cut" due to its encircling nature, involved deploying a decoy army along the Maginot Line, while the main attack was planned through Belgium and the Netherlands to the north, bypassing the Maginot Line altogether. On May 10, 1940, German troops crossed into French borders and advanced toward Paris within just five days. By June 25, when France signed the armistice, the defensive structures of the Maginot Line paradoxically remained intact.

In chess, beginners are cautioned against bringing their Queen out too early, as it becomes vulnerable to being encircled and trapped easily.

Flanking attack

The third offensive strategy is the flanking attack, aimed at applying pressure to the sides of the enemy front to force them into retreat. The attacker gains ground while the enemy front falls into disarray and chaos. Such a strategy allows for avoiding direct confrontation and the significant loss of resources. However, it comes with the drawback of diverting valuable resources from the core business, thus potentially making the attacker more vulnerable to frontal assaults.

In business terms, a flanking attack involves competing in a market segment that the defender does not consider critical. It also entails a subtle and discreet promotional campaign. Tailoring a product for the specific niche being targeted can complement this strategy.

The flanking attack strategy is recommended when:

- The market is segmented, with some segments underserved by competitors.
- The target competitor is well-defended and could easily repel a frontal attack.
- The attacker possesses relatively strong resources.

An exemplary instance of a flanking attack in business is Tesla's introduction of electric vehicles. This strategic move enabled Tesla to penetrate the automotive market by appealing to the underserved segment of environmentally conscious consumers and tech enthusiasts seeking alternatives to traditional internal combustion engine vehicles.

In chess, flanking attacks are frequently seen even in the opening phase. They often occur in positions where players have castled on opposite sides, each attacking the flank where the opponent has castled. Flanking attacks also manifest in positions with pawn chains, where the attack targets the base of the chain, typically located on one side of the chessboard.

In military strategy, every encirclement of the enemy begins with an attack on the flank. Therefore, all the previous examples mentioned as encirclements could also be classified as instances of the flanking attack strategy.

Guerrilla

In the field of marketing, the guerrilla strategy is an expression coined by American publicist Jay Conrad Levinson in 1984[5] to describe a form of unconventional, low-cost advertising. It involves creatively aggressive tactics that target the imaginative and psychological mechanisms of end users. Guerrilla marketing is an ideal tool for entrepreneurs with limited advertising budgets. Promotion efforts emphasize time, energy, and creativity over financial resources. Public attention is captured through highly original, sometimes provocative events.

In chess, guerrilla tactics are quantitatively theorized. Examples include playing against an opponent with a significantly higher ELO rating or when facing a material disadvantage against an opponent of similar strength.

Let's consider the scenario of playing against an opponent with a significantly higher ELO rating. For those unfamiliar with this metric, the ELO rating system calculates the relative strength of players. The difference in ratings between two players predicts the match outcome. After each game, the winning player gains points from the losing player, with the points calculated based on the pre-game ELO difference. Here are some key facts about the ELO rating system:

- Magnus Carlsen's current ELO rating is 2832 versus Alphazero's 3300. Carlsen held the world champion title from 2013 to 2023 and remains the strongest human player by ELO.
- A player with a rating 200 points higher than their opponent's is expected to win 76% of the time.

Another fundamental assumption is that each player's chess performance in a game is a normally distributed random variable. Thus, a player's strength can be represented as a bell curve. The magic of statistics lies in the fact that even a lower-rated player has some chance of winning against a stronger opponent.

Let's consider two players 1 and 2, with strengths measured as ELO1 and ELO2, respectively, where ELO1 and ELO2 will be the mean values, i.e. the central points where their Gaussian curves peak, while σ_1 and σ_2 denote the standard deviations, i.e. the widths of the curves.

We can observe that on the right side of the chart, Player 1's curve rises above Player 2's curve. This area represents where Player 1, despite being weaker on average, has a chance to win the game.

We can also see that if we increase the standard deviations (chart on the right in Figure 4.1), the area where the weaker player can win will expand.

Thus, the general strategy involves increasing the standard deviation for the weaker player, while reducing it for the stronger player. In essence, the guerrilla strategy for the weaker player is to amplify the game's standard deviations. How can we do this?

In chess, we can increase the standard deviation by introducing confusion and complicating the position on the chessboard. Positions that are highly unbalanced and tactical tend to exhibit a greater standard deviation compared to straightforward, linear positions.

Conversely, the stronger player typically aims to simplify the position and exchange pieces, thereby reducing tension and avoiding risky positions.

These strategies are applicable beyond chess, encompassing realms such as business and military tactics. In business, Levinson extensively illustrates these strategies in his seminal work.

Remember this key point: when you find yourself at a disadvantage, increase the sigma by muddying the waters and creating confusion.

In military contexts, notable instances of guerrilla include some of the Roman Empire's defeats, often at the hands of ostensibly weaker adversaries who leveraged their terrain advantageously, creating complications

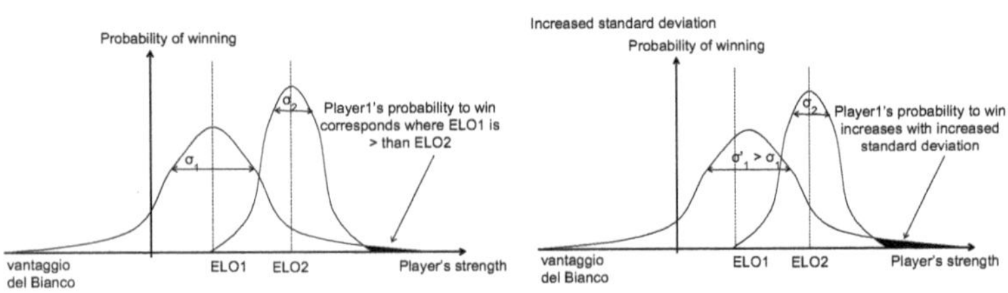

Figure 4.1 How to use standard deviation to increase our chances of winning a game

and confusion on the battlefields (increasing the standard deviation). For instance, the Germans in the dense forests of Teutoburg and the Samnites in the rugged mountain passes of the Caudine Forks created challenging combat environments that proved detrimental to Roman forces.

Defensive strategies

Offensive strategies require the opponent to implement effective defensive strategies in order to avoid defeat.

In this paragraph, we will concentrate on three types of defensive strategies: positional, mobile, and counterattack.

Positional defense

Positional defense involves protecting a fortified position by introducing barriers to entry around products, brands, and market segments. Typical actions include strengthening brand equity, customer loyalty and satisfaction, exclusivity in distribution contracts, and protecting patents and trademarks. It is typically implemented in situations where the defender has a dominant market position, and potential attackers have limited resources. However, it tends to be a weak defense because the one who adopts it becomes an easy target. This can lead to a siege situation.

Positional defense played a crucial role in World War I, where it became synonymous with trench warfare and the establishment of fortified positions. A notable example is the Italian Front in the Alps, where both Italian and Austro-Hungarian forces established extensive defenses. This included constructing trenches, barbed wire, and fortified positions, leading to a grueling and static form of warfare.

In business strategy, examples of positional defense include:

- Patents and intellectual property, as seen in the pharmaceutical sector, which prevent competitors from producing generic versions and thereby maintain a competitive edge.
- Exclusive distribution agreements with high-end retailers, a common strategy among luxury brands.
- Proprietary logistics networks, such as Amazon's, which allow for full control over marketing and distribution strategies.
- Continuous innovation, a hallmark of innovative businesses like Apple and Google.

In chess, the rise of positional defense signaled the decline of the romantic era characterized by dazzling and imaginative sacrifices. This shift occurred in the late 19th century with Wilhelm Steinitz, who pioneered the initial principles of positional play. This approach swiftly established itself as a more stable and effective style, countering the flamboyant yet risky and often incorrect nature of romantic combinations.

Mobile defense

Mobile defense involves the constant redeployment of resources and the continuous development of new strategies and tactics. It aims to create a moving target that is difficult to attack. The defender develops flexible reaction mechanisms to respond to attacks.

In business terms, mobile defense involves strategies that keep a company dynamic and elusive, making it difficult for competitors to target effectively. This approach necessitates a flexible organization with strong capabilities in marketing, product development, and market intelligence. For instance, Apple's relentless product innovation creates a constantly shifting landscape that competitors find challenging to attack. Similarly, Netflix's ongoing content creation ensures its offerings remain fresh and appealing, making it difficult for competitors to keep up.

In military history, a notable example of mobile defense is the Roman Empire's army. Instead of stationing their forces solely along the Empire's vast borders (limes), which would have required an enormous number of soldiers, the Romans implemented a more flexible strategy. They positioned some of their legions centrally within the Empire, allowing them to be quickly deployed to any border area under attack. This approach enabled rapid response to external threats, maintaining effective defense with fewer resources.

Finally, in chess, players like Anatoly Karpov are celebrated for their skill in maneuvering pieces to optimal squares, ensuring a solid yet flexible defensive position. This technique involves subtle piece movements that enhance the position without committing to a specific plan too early.

Counter attack

Attack is the best defense. When you're under pressure in a battle, it's effective to counterattack against the opponent's weakest point. The main challenge with this technique is psychological, as mental inertia and fatigue from prolonged defense—whether in chess, military confrontations, or market competition—make it difficult to shift from defense to offense.

A successful example of a counteroffensive was the launch of Piaggio's three-wheeled scooter, the MP3, in 2003. At that time, European scooter manufacturers were struggling against Asian competitors who were steadily eroding their market share with new models and lower costs. Another example is the rivalry between Coca-Cola and Pepsi, where each new product launch or marketing effort by one side is consistently countered by the other.

Chapter 4—Strategic planning—interviews

Luca Desiata interviewed by Bachar Kouatly

What types of frontal attacks have you experienced in your professional life, whether you were the attacker or defender?

The most violent frontal attack I experienced was during my tenure as CEO of Sogin. On a critical project to mitigate the environmental hazard from highly radioactive liquid waste stored in northern Italy, the main contractor decided to abandon the construction site and sue us for €60 million, alleging failures in project supervision. This contractor, a major Italian engineering company with substantial influence and financial resources, launched a multifaceted attack, including political pressure, legal action, and a smear campaign in the media. My defensive resources were limited due to the company's bylaws and internal regulations, which indirectly restricted spending on media and legal matters. Consequently, our defense strategy focused on a detailed analysis of the project's dynamics to counter the rationale behind the €60 million claim on a project estimated to be worth €100 million upon completion. The court case dragged on for years and was still unresolved when my term ended. Recently, I learned that the preliminary outcome of the trial was somewhat favorable to my company, validating the strength of our positional defense.

Do you have any other examples where you were the attacker?

In 2014, I founded pptArt, the world's first crowdsourcing platform for art projects. This innovative idea applied the concept of crowdsourcing to the art world for the first time, challenging some foundational principles of contemporary art. The art crowdsourcing process begins with the client providing a detailed document, known as a brief, similar to corporate communication practices. This brief is then shared with our platform of over 4,000 artists from 74 countries. Artists who feel inspired by the project submit creative proposals, usually in the form of a sketch along with a price tag. Instead of visiting numerous art galleries, clients can comfortably review all the proposals and select the one that best meets the criteria outlined in the brief. PptArt then assigns a contract to the chosen artist and oversees the artwork's execution until delivery to the client.

The revolutionary aspect of this methodology lies in the inspiration behind the creation of new artwork. In the contemporary art world, the artist's personal inspiration typically drives the creation of artwork, which they then try to sell, often with limited success. In contrast, the art crowdsourcing process is driven by the specific needs of a client, which the artist then interprets through their personal style. Additionally, this method revolutionizes the concept of art's value. In contemporary art, value is often seen as ephemeral and difficult to determine mechanically. However, in the art crowdsourcing process, artists submit price proposals, enabling the creation of demand-supply curves. The intersection of these curves determines a price equilibrium, representing the value of the art project.

Everything was objectively very interesting and clients were enthused by the richness of proposals and the transparency of the crowdsourcing sale process compared to the opacity of art dealers and galleries.

The problem came, somewhat expectedly by the art world which felt threatened and tried to boycott us. As the pptArt team did not come from the art world but from corporate creative agencies, we needed to define how to gain our space in this world. The strategy involved a mix of guerrilla tactics and more structured attacks. Given that the crowdsourcing process recognizes relevance to the clients' needs over the artists' interpretation, we decided to ride this distinctive wave and to organize our offensive around the role of art clients. Within this strategy, we organized the first Corporate Art exhibit in 2015 at the Galleria Nazionale d'Arte Moderna in Rome with the aim to give visibility and recognition to art patrons in the corporate world. This first initiative proved so successful that we decided to raise the bar.

Under the patronage of the Italian Ministry of Art and Culture, pptArt organized the first Corporate Art Awards in 2016, aiming to recognize and honor art patrons within the corporate world. Among 80 participating companies from 22 countries, Banca Intesa Sanpaolo and Deutsche Bank were awarded for the best corporate collections, American Express for its international restoration program, Shiseido for the oldest corporate collection in Japan, and Piaggio for its social media campaign supporting its corporate museum.

In 2017, the Corporate Art Awards expanded to include the institutional sector, and the program was renamed "Mecenati of the XXI Century" to acknowledge outstanding art projects supported by both corporations and institutions. This broader event was hosted at the Quirinal Palace by the President of the Italian Republic.

The 2018 edition of the "Mecenati of the XXI Century" Awards took place at the European Parliament in Brussels under the auspices of President Antonio Tajani. This third edition significantly enhanced pptArt's international reputation within the art world.

The three editions of the Awards had seen the participation of over 200 companies and institutions from 28 countries.

This experience proves that even smaller players can deliver powerful attacks to market leaders, by leveraging innovative features and thinking big.

Anatoly Karpov interviewed by Bachar Kouatly

What is strategic planning in chess?

Strategic planning in chess does not differ substantially from a business approach. A chess player starts with an exploratory analysis of the current situation, evaluates the pros and cons of the various alternatives, sets targets after the analysis of multiple scenarios, and evaluates the threats and the alternatives available to his opponent.

Chess positions are magmatic, both at the level of the mental stages, which lead the player to make a move, and at the level of the evolution on the chessboard through successive stages whose strategic contents change at every move. The themes in a position evolve along multiple layers. It's like a multidimensional space where ideas collide and connect in a dynamic way.

What's your primary goal in a position? Finding a winning plan or move?

To borrow a meaningful expression from my second Furman,[6] I would say that the primary goal in a position is to look for a plan that will make us at least not lose!

Generally speaking, we should always aim to find continuations toward positions in which we feel at our ease, where we can anticipate intellectual comfort and pleasure.

Given the strong similarities with the business planning process, do chess players use such corporate tools as the strengths-weaknesses-opportunities-threats (SWOT) matrix and strategy canvas?

No, we do not. Chess practice is not so structured as the corporate world where managers need to share ideas and concepts among many corporate functions, often located in different continents. Normally, the chess champion works with a small circle of trusted collaborators. The exchange of concepts and ideas with these collaborators is purely verbal and is immediately tested on the board in case of disagreement. Alternatively, chess software can be used as a sparring partner with no emotional or psychological involvement. This is particularly useful when human chess players tend to "fall in love" with the wrong moves and need an objective cold shower.

What would come out from the application of business tools to the chess world? The SWOT analysis, for example.

It would be an absolutely consistent exercise. Like a manager in a business situation, a chess player analyzes a position taking into consideration strengths and weaknesses, threats and opportunities. Any chess manual is organized around these four key variables.

What if we applied the SWOT matrix to a chess position?

Let's take for example the Italian opening, one of the first openings ever to be studied with a scientific approach. The main position of the variation is reached after the following moves[7] (Figure 4.2):

1 e4; e5
2 Nf3; Nc6
3 Bc4; Bc5
4 c3; Nf6
5 d4; exd
6 cxd; Bb4 +
7 Bd2; Bxd2 +
8 Nbxd2; d5
9 exd; Nxd5
10 0-0; 0-0
11 Qb3; Nce7
12 a4; c6

This is a well-known opening, one of the first to be historically developed in the context of the theory of chess and one of the first to be taught to beginners due to the linearity of its strategic issues. We can summarize White's key strategic factors in a SWOT matrix as follows (Table 4.1).

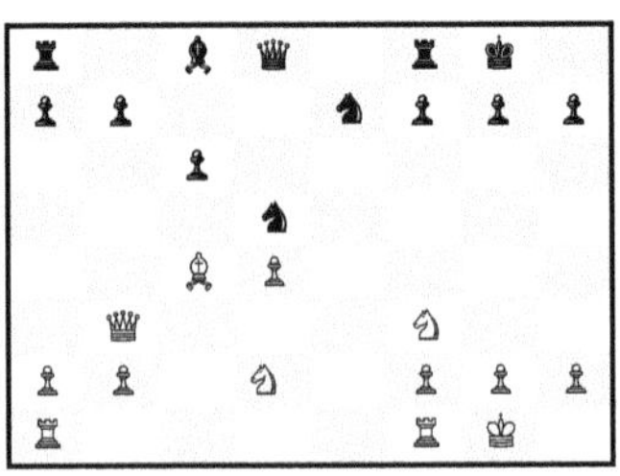

Figure 4.2 Typical position of the Italian opening[8]

Table 4.1 Karpov's SWOT analysis of a position from the Italian game

Strengths	**Weaknesses**
Advantage of space and maneuver C and E columns ready to be occupied C5 and e5 outposts available for White Knights	Isolated d4 pawn D5 outpost controlled by Black Weakness of the first rank
Opportunities	**Threats**
Increase pressure on the pawns on the Queen side, especially the pawn in b7. If Black plays b6 to defend, then switch the attack on c6 Attack the opponent's King on the weak points f7 and h7. Checkmate threats on the eighth rank	The risk is that Black can reorganize quickly his forces and nullify White's space advantage Transition to the ending. The ending is lost for White because of the weakness of the d4 pawn Mating threats on the first rank

How can the SWOT matrix support the development of a chess strategy?

The strategy follows as a natural consequence from the above analysis. Clearly we have different possibilities to choose from, according to our preferences and style.

As White, we can adopt an incremental strategy, gradually improving our position (e.g. occupying the open columns with the Rooks or the central outposts with the Knights). As it is shown in the "threats" quadrant of the SWOT matrix, the risk is that Black can reorganize his forces quickly, nullifying White's space advantage. Therefore, the price of a move is much higher for White than for Black. White absolutely cannot afford to waste time.

White can decide to launch a direct attack against the Black King, placing the Knights, the Bishop, and the Queen against the opponent's castling. Alternatively, the attack can be launched against lower value targets such as the pawns on the Black Queen's side.

Notes

1 M. E. Porter. How Competitive Forces Shape Strategy. *Harvard Business Review*, 1979.
2 We'll disregard the fifth force, "internal competition", as it is less relevant to our current analysis.
3 https://www.theguardian.com/science/2004/mar/04/2.
4 https://militaryfamilies.com/sports/chess-helps-marines-train-for-battle/.
5 J. C. Levinson. *Guerrilla Marketing: Easy and Inexpensive Strategies for Making Big Profits from Your Small Business* (Piatkus, 2007).
6 Furman Semen Abramovich, International Grandmaster and Karpov's coach between 1969 and 1978.
7 Chessboards drawn using Unicode chess pieces by piliapp.com.
8 Chessboards drawn using Unicode chess pieces by piliapp.com

Chapter 5

Risk management

After defining a strategic objective through an intensive mental process and allocating resources based on the military strategy's nature, managers and chess players alike must prepare to face the reality and acknowledge the risk that implementation may not unfold according to their well-structured mental plans. Risk is actually defined as a factor that may threaten the success of a project or the achievement of a goal.

According to the international standard ISO 31000, risk management involves "the identification, evaluation, and prioritization of risks… with the objective of controlling the probability or impact of unfortunate events".

The crucial aspect of this definition is the control of probability, making risk management closely connected to statistics. When dealing with statistics, the game of dice naturally comes to mind, whereas chess, with its deterministic nature, might seem unrelated. However, there is a crucial distinction in how risk is approached between chess and dice: the dice players do not actively select the risk profile of the game they want to play, unlike the risk manager and the chess player. From a risk assessment perspective, the decision-making process of a risk manager when selecting a specific option or a financial manager when selecting an investment option mirrors the strategic considerations of chess players when choosing the risk profile of their moves.

Risk management in corporate settings

Generally, corporate risk management is structured around a risk-appetite framework, based on a dashboard that highlights the primary risks identified for the company. Each risk is linked to an indicator with a threshold and an escalation protocol to address situations when the threshold is exceeded.

Thresholds are often established by considering the historical trend ±2 standard deviations, signaling when a particular risk is rising significantly compared to historical patterns.

DOI: 10.4324/9781003533719-5

In project management, contemporary software goes beyond deterministic approaches that rely on a limited number of scenarios (pessimistic, optimistic, base). Instead, it allows project managers to associate a statistical curve with each variable, such as the cost and duration of activities in the Gantt chart, thereby encompassing a vast array of scenarios.

Risk management in finance

Risk management holds particular relevance in finance as it seeks to reduce uncertainty in investment decisions. In finance, risk management revolves around the relationship between risk and return. The guiding principle is clear: higher risk demands higher returns, whereas lower risk results in lower returns. Return on a financial asset is defined as the ratio of initial capital to the profits generated from investment or trading activities within a specific timeframe. Risk can be defined as the degree of uncertainty in the market regarding the actual realization of expected returns, usually quantified mathematically as the variance (standard deviation) of the expected returns.

The modern portfolio theory, introduced by Markowitz in 1952,[1] offers the most widely accepted formalization of how risk and return interact. This theory provides a mathematical framework for constructing a portfolio of assets that maximizes expected return for a given level of risk. In this framework, financial investors are deemed rational when, for a given level of return, they select a portfolio with lower risk. Conversely, if presented with a specific level of risk, they choose a portfolio with a higher return.

An investment option is typically characterized by two variables: R for returns and σ for variance, which represents the volatility of returns and serves as a measure of risk.

An immediate corollary from these definitions is the principle of portfolio diversification: investors can reduce portfolio risk simply by holding combinations of instruments that are negatively correlated. This statement can be demonstrated as follows: let's consider a portfolio consisting of 30% of stock A and 70% of stock B, where A and B are two stocks with returns R_A and R_B, variances σ_A and σ_B, and correlation ρ_{AB}. The portfolio's return and variance are given by:

$$\text{Portfolio return} = 30\%\ R_A + 70\%\ R_B$$

$$\text{Variance of the portfolio } \sigma^2_p = (30\%)^2 \times \sigma^2_A + (70\%)^2 \times \sigma^2_B + 2\text{x}\ (30\%) \times (70\%) \times \sigma_A \times \sigma_B \times \rho_{AB}$$

It is clear from the second formula on the portfolio variance that if the correlation ρ_{AB} between the two stocks is negative, the variance of the portfolio will be lower than those of the two stocks A and B due to the negative contribution of the term 2 x (30%) × (70%) × $\sigma_A \times \sigma_B \times \rho_{AB}$, where ρ_{AB} is negative by definition. An example of two businesses with negative correlation would be an umbrella manufacturer and a sunscreen company. When it rains frequently, umbrella sales increase while sunscreen sales tend to decrease.

These variables, returns and variance, are also central to the Black–Scholes model, which is used for calculating the prices of options and derivatives.

Decision-trees applied to finance

A quantitative explanation of the relation between risk-return can be given by the binomial trees. Binomial trees have a double advantage: on one side, they represent a particular case of the Black & Scholes equation for the pricing of options and, on the other side, are immediately comparable to chess decision-trees, which we have discussed in detail in the chapter on decision-making processes.

Suppose you have a stock whose starting price is \$100 and whose historical monthly volatility is 1%, in other words, the price of the stock in one month either rises by 1\$ or drops by 1\$ (it is called a binomial tree because it represents price movements of equal value either up or down). For simplicity, an upward movement in one month followed by a downward movement the next month, and vice versa, is rounded to zero.

Assuming that historical volatility can predict future movements, the share price will be either \$101 or \$99 after a month, with an equal 50% probability for each outcome. Thus, we can determine the potential share prices for each subsequent month. Figure 5.1 illustrates the possible price trends over the next four months, starting in April 2012.

What is the probability that after four months the share price drops below \$97 and how much should be the cost of the insurance to cover the risk?

On the right axis, the possible occurrences of a given price in August are displayed as a histogram. For instance, reaching \$104 requires following a single path of continuous monthly increases, represented by the topmost branch of the tree. Conversely, reaching \$102 can be achieved through four different paths: up-up-up-down, up-up-down-up, up-down-up-up, and down-up-up-up. By exploring all the paths leading to prices of \$100, \$98, and \$96, you'll find that the occurrences are 6, 4, and 1, respectively. This resulting histogram resembles a Gaussian or bell-shaped curve and tends to become more continuous as the granularity of the variations increases, such as by considering daily

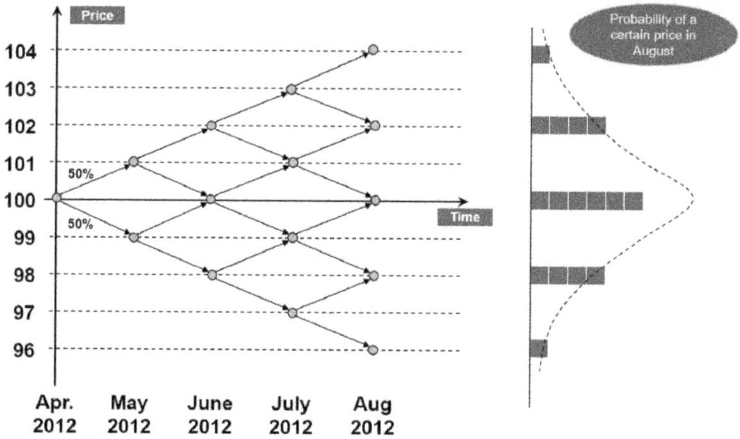

Figure 5.1 Binomial tree to predict price probability

variations instead of monthly. This method employs a binomial tree as an approximation of the Black–Scholes equation, producing a Gaussian curve.

Now, it is simple to determine the probability that the price will fall below $97 in August. We count the occurrences where the price is below $97 (one case in this instance) and divide it by the total number of possible occurrences (1 + 4 + 6 + 4 + 1 = 16). Therefore, the probability for the price to drop below $97 in August is 1/16.

This visual representation of the tree also illustrates why volatility is associated with risk: if volatility increases from 1% to 2%, the tree structure doubles in width, and the probability of the price dropping below $97 in August increases to 5/16. This higher volatility implies greater risk but also the potential for higher gains, as the tree remains symmetrical and the same probabilities apply to the threshold price above $103.

It's important to note that the assumption that historical volatility predicts future outcomes is not accurate. However, because the future is unpredictable, it is valuable to adopt a reasonable assumption that allows us to perform calculations, providing a sense of control over future events.

Investment opportunities with low risk and high returns typically attract investments until the risk-return profile converges toward the average. For example, if a company's stock is undervalued, investors will buy shares until the rising price aligns with the expected risk-return profile of the business.

Risk management in chess

The concept of financial risk and return is a fundamental part of a chess player's mindset. To illustrate this equivalence, let's consider the two chess positions in Figure 5.2, which result from Black's possible responses to White's initial move e4 (King's pawn advancing two squares).

The "character" of the two positions is visually intuitive, even for those who are not chess experts.

The chessboard on the left depicts the exchange variation of the French Defense: a symmetrical, balanced position without significant tensions.

The chessboard on the right depicts the Najdorf variation of the Sicilian Defense. This results in an asymmetric and unbalanced position, where the opponents' pieces are in close contact, creating palpable tension.

These visual impressions are confirmed by practical experience and game statistics. According to a database of about 2 million games played over the last 150 years,[2] the exchange variation of the French Defense shows a significant tendency (36%) to result in draws, whereas the draw probability in the Najdorf variation drops to only 23%, as shown in Table 5.1. Playing the Najdorf offers a higher chance of a decisive result: a better chance of winning, but also a higher risk of losing.

Similar considerations apply when a chess player makes a move in the middle game. If the chess engine evaluates the move at +0.5 (an advantage equivalent to half a pawn, with a conventional value of 1), this does not necessarily mean the game is won. The positive evaluation represents only the mean value of a broader range of possible outcomes. The width of this range depends on the complexity of the position. Linear and balanced positions tend to have narrower ranges, concentrated closer to the mean value, making them more predictable. In contrast, unbalanced and

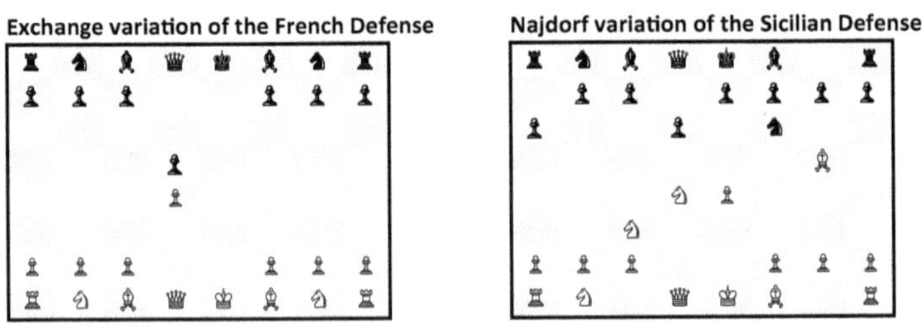

Figure 5.2 Two chess positions.[3]

Table 5.1 Winning probabilities for two chess variations

Result	*French—exchange variation*	*French—all variations*	*Sicilian—all variations*	*Sicilian—Najdorf variation with Bg5*
1-0 (White wins)	29%	39%	37%	39%
½-½ (draw)	36%	30%	28%	23%
0–1 (Black wins)	35%	31%	35%	38%
Number of games in the database	40,000	292,000	851,000	23,700

complex positions exhibit wider ranges, indicating greater uncertainty in the evaluation.

Chess and Kahneman's theory of irrational investors

The entire theory of traditional finance, which assumes rational investors, was challenged by an observed contradiction in human behavior: people are willing to travel across a city to take advantage of a promotional sale offering a 50-euro discount on an item of clothing priced at 150 euros. However, they are unwilling to make the same effort to save the same amount when buying a car priced at 9,100 euros instead of 9,150 euros. When confronted with two investments that offer the same benefit in absolute terms, consumers exhibit two different behaviors, thereby violating classical utility theory.

This observation prompted Kahneman to develop prospect theory,[4] also known as the theory of irrational investors, primarily based on the behaviors exhibited in tests involving the following two choices:

1 Given the choice between (1) receiving $3,000 immediately or (2) paying $200 to participate in a lottery where one can win $4,000 with an 80% probability, most people prefer option 1, despite both options being equivalent from the perspective of a rational investor.
2 Having to choose between (1) losing $1,000 now or (2) playing a lottery in which one has a 90% chance of not losing anything and 10% of losing $10,000, the majority of preferences will go to the option 2 though the two options are equivalent from the point of view of the rational investor.

These behaviors indicate that investors are not entirely rational in their decision-making but rather exhibit a propensity or aversion to risk depending on how choices and options are framed. These tendencies can be summarized as follows:

- A tendency toward risk aversion when presented with a certain gain.
- A tendency toward risk-taking when faced with a certain loss.

The implications and applications of these mechanisms in the financial realm were formalized by Kahneman in prospect theory, contributing to his winning the Nobel Prize in Economics in 2002.

These dynamics are not confined to the financial sector but can also be applied to other aspects of life, such as chess. Let's consider a chess position where, based on the engine evaluation, White's position is assessed at −5. This indicates that Black has an advantage of 5 pawns (conventionally valued at 1), which is normally enough to win the game. What strategy should White employ to prevent Black from solidifying this advantage and aiming for an endgame such an advantage could easily lead to victory?

Similar to the guerrilla warfare strategy discussed earlier, when White faces a material disadvantage of −5, the best approach is to increase the variance as follows: complicate and confuse the situation, create ambiguity, intensify the pressure, and avoid simplifications to keep more pieces in play that can generate further complications.

As depicted in Figure 5.3, two positions with equal mean value (−5 for White, indicating a 5-pawn disadvantage) are represented by bell-shaped curves centered around the same value of −5. These curves illustrate different probabilities of White still winning the game despite the disadvantage. By increasing the variance (i.e. the width of the curve) from σ to σ′, one enhances the probability of the White player winning

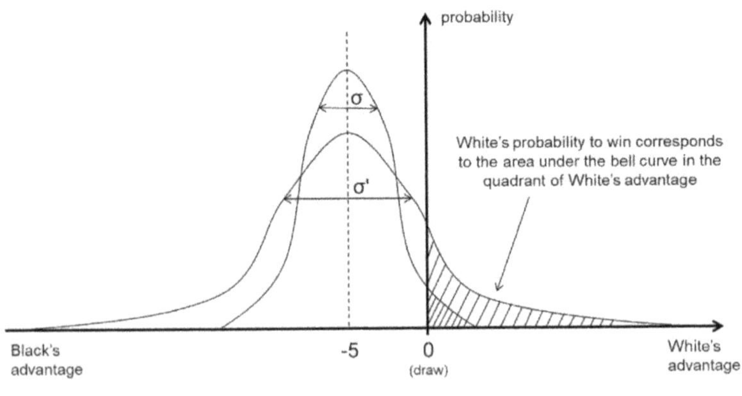

Figure 5.3 Winning probabilities in two positions with the equal mean value

despite the −5 disadvantage (White's chances of winning are represented by the area under the bell curve in the right quadrant, which shows White's advantage).

If White is at −5, the zero-sum nature of chess means that Black, perceiving their position as +5, will adopt an opposite strategy to capitalize on this advantage and aim for victory. Instead of taking additional risks, Black will focus on exchanging pieces to reduce the tension and to transition to the endgame quickly, countering any attempts by White to complicate the position. This cautious strategy is intended to secure the conversion of the advantage into a win.

In conclusion, we can assert that the two principles underlying Kahneman's theory of the irrational investor (a tendency toward risk aversion when presented with a sure gain, and a tendency toward risk-taking when faced with a sure loss) can be observed in a game of chess, particularly in the behaviors of Black and White players when confronted with highly unbalanced positions.

Therefore, Kahneman's theory of the irrational investor could indeed have been validated in the realm of chess, by analyzing the statistics of moves chosen by players in highly unbalanced positions, thus potentially saving Kahneman the effort and costs of organizing controlled studies.

In general, chess databases, containing millions of games and as many corresponding moves/decisions, represent an undervalued treasure trove of human decisions that could be highly valuable for cognitive and behavioral science studies.

Chapter 5—Risk management—interviews

Luca Desiata interviewed by Bachar Kouatly

What types of risk management experience have you encountered in your professional career?

My initial risk management projects were in credit management between 1998 and 2001, when I was a strategy consultant with one of the top three strategy consultancies. During this period, I developed credit risk management models for several Italian banks. At that time, credit risk management software did not exist, so we created models using Excel spreadsheets integrated with statistical tools, which can be considered forerunners of modern credit risk management automated tools. The input for these models was the banks' credit lists, and the output was VAR (Value at Risk), based on specific risk assumptions for each credit category modeled with statistical curves. In addition to the quantitative models, the projects also included the definition and implementation of credit risk management processes, frameworks, and systems.

In 2009, as Head of International Strategy for the Italian multinational electricity producer, I developed a comprehensive financial model for the entire company. This model assessed the variation of the company's share price following changes in strategic variables (e.g. oil prices, €/$ exchange rate). Using sensitivity analysis, I supported the development of the company's hedging strategy against major financial risks.

Between 2011 and 2013, as the Project Manager for the construction of the Flamanville 3 nuclear plant in France on behalf of the Italian multinational electricity producer, I managed operational risk on a multi-billion-euro construction project.

From 2016 to 2019, as CEO of Sogin, I helped redefine global standards for project management in nuclear decommissioning in collaboration with the IAEA (International Atomic Energy Agency). This new approach involved using statistical curves for each variable in the decommissioning plan. The variance (width) of these curves was based on a database of historical activities in the same technical area, comparing planned versus actual data. As the oldest nuclear decommissioning company among G7 countries due to the 1987 referendum against nuclear energy, Sogin had the world's richest historical database of nuclear decommissioning activities, providing a competitive advantage in accurately estimating variances directly related to the risk of each activity.

Finally, from 2022 to 2024, as Head of Risk Management at the Italian subsidiary of a major credit card company, I contributed to strengthening the supervision of credit and operational risks of the company within the Bank of Italy's regulatory framework as well as the guidelines of the American headquarters.

All these examples demonstrate that risk management is a crucial corporate activity across all industrial sectors and at every level of seniority.

Anatoly Karpov interviewed by Bachar Kouatly

What is risk in chess?

Those who do not dare will not win. Risk is the essence of chess, central to the pleasure of playing the game.

Who is exposed to a higher risk? The attacker or the defender?

When I sacrifice a piece for an attack, I take the risk that my attack might fail and my opponent will launch a winning counteroffensive. Conversely, my opponent takes a risk by accepting my sacrifice, facing the possibility that my attack will overwhelm them. The question is not "Who is taking the risk?" but "Which of the two risks is bigger?"

Let me give you an example from the fourth game of my last world title challenge against Kasparov in New York. It was a Spanish opening where Kasparov, playing White, sacrificed three pawns for a fierce attack on my King. This left me with a four-pawn advantage on the queenside, sufficient for an easy win in the endgame if his attack failed. I found myself in a situation where my defense had to be extremely precise—every move had to be perfect, as the slightest mistake would be fatal. The strategies of attack and defense balanced each other perfectly throughout the game, creating a prolonged situation of high risk and immense pressure on both sides. The clash of the two armies ended in a draw, an ideal result to preserve the perfect dynamic equilibrium of that game.

What factors influence the appetite for risk?

The main factor is your personal inclination to take or avoid risks. Over time, every chess player develops a preference for certain positions where they feel more or less comfortable.

However, many subjective and objective factors influence one's appetite for risk.

If you are in time trouble ("zeitnot" in chess jargon), you will tend to simplify the position to avoid risks. Conversely, if your opponent is in time trouble, you will tend to complicate the position to put pressure on them and increase their likelihood of making a mistake.

If you have a clear advantage, you will tend to simplify the position to minimize risks. If you are at a disadvantage, you will try to complicate the position to jeopardize your opponent's chances of victory.

If you need to win a game to earn points in a tournament, you will be more likely to take risks and enter unbalanced positions.

If you play against a computer you will tend to avoid risks as you know that every uncertainty for you is a certain victory for the computer.

Finally, the historical period in which we live also affects our appetite for risk. Nowadays, no one would play the high-risk variations and bold sacrifices that were popular in the 19th century. Advances in chess theory and defensive techniques have rendered these variations obsolete.

What have computers changed in the approach to risk?

In my view, computers have profoundly influenced our approach to risk by significantly reducing the uncertainty in evaluating various positions. In statistical terms, we can say that computers have reduced the "variance" when evaluating a particular move. They have even revealed the correct solutions to certain endgames, challenging and surpassing centuries of human study and analysis that had been unable to provide definitive conclusions.

Against computers, we can't afford even the smallest mistake. The general advice is to play cautiously and opt for low-risk variations, as the psychological impact and surprise of bold sacrifices have no effect on their unemotional intelligence. Computers have greatly improved our ability to manage risk.

Can you give us an example that demonstrates how the chess player's approach to risk is similar to that of a financial investor?

I am sure that Kahneman would have liked Polugaevsky's[5] asymmetric style of play as an additional example for his theory of the irrational investor.

Let's see how Polugaevsky would behave when playing chess.

With White, he used to play normal variations.

As Black, he would dive into highly unbalanced and reckless variations, fearing that playing conventionally would lead to a slow defeat.

This asymmetric behavior can be explained as Polugaevsky's attempt to counter White's "first mover's advantage" that will be estimated at 10% in the chapter on negotiations of this book as the statistical difference between White's and Black's victories from a database of 4 million games. The graph illustrates the value of Black's starting position (–0.1 for Black or +0.1 for White) with σ as the level of risk (Figure 5.4).

To offset his initial disadvantage with Black, Polugayevski wisely opted to increase the risks by diving into unbalanced variations, aiming to shift the variance from σ to σ' and thereby improve his chances of winning with Black despite White's first mover's advantage.

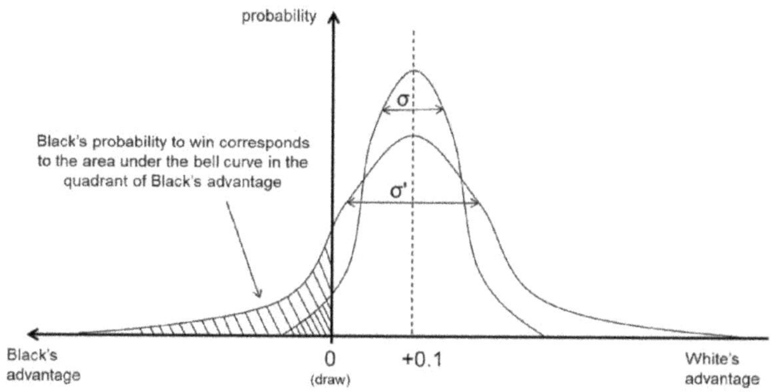

Figure 5.4 How to increase winning probabilities

Do you have any insights into why many chess players have recently transitioned to poker? Is this shift related to the differing risk-return profiles of the two games?

I would argue that this phenomenon is more related to the return on investment rather than the risk-return profile. Compared to chess, poker players can potentially earn significant sums with relatively less time spent on study and preparation. While poker does provide interesting intellectual challenges related to probability and risk management, I am personally less attracted to it because the strategic element is somewhat influenced by luck, and the short game cycles offer less opportunity for deep, sophisticated enjoyment.

What is the riskiest move you have ever played? What was the result?

I have always favored traditional variations, making solid and consistent moves even in uncertain positions. I take risks only after careful analysis and precise calculation. Unbalanced variations and inherently flawed strategies are not part of my playing style or comfort zone. I avoid them even in blitz games against weaker opponents and never seek shortcuts.

Notes

1 H. M. Markowitz. Portfolio Selection. *The Journal of Finance*, 1952.
2 www.chessgames.com. Data elaborated by the author.
3 Both chessboards are drawn using Unicode chess pieces by piliapp.com
4 D. Kahneman, A. Tversky, Prospect Theory: An Analysis of Decision Under Risk *Econometrica*, 1979.
5 Lev Polugaevsky, International Grandmaster, challenger for the world title several times.

Chapter 6

Negotiations

Chess and the cold war

> The key flashpoints of the Cold War are fairly obvious: Berlin, Cuba, Vietnam, Korea. But Reykjavik? In 1972 it played host to the most surreal of all Cold War confrontations: the battle between Bobby Fischer and Boris Spassky to be world chess champion.

This is how Kenan Malik began his 2007 article in *The Telegraph*.[1]

The negotiations on the chessboard between Fischer and Spassky mirrored the political negotiations between US President Richard Nixon and the General Secretary of the Communist Party of the USSR, Leonid Brezhnev. 1972 was not only the year of the Fischer–Spassky match but also the year when the Soviet Union achieved nuclear parity with the United States. A few months before the World Chess Championship began, Nixon traveled to Beijing to thaw relations with Mao Zedong and also signed the ABM Treaty with Brezhnev to limit the proliferation of strategic offensive arms.

The Fischer–Spassky match took place at a time when the first signs of improvement between the two blocs began to appear. When Fischer, increasingly uncooperative, forfeited the second game, jeopardizing the championship, Henry Kissinger did not hesitate to interrupt the Vietnam War peace negotiations. He picked up the phone and called Fischer, saying, "This is the worst chess player calling the best chess player in the world". Fortunately, Kissinger, who had studied game theory at Harvard, managed to persuade Fischer to return to the board by using the famous patriotic line, "America wants you to go over there and beat the Russians". Fischer returned, won the championship against Spassky and became a national hero. A year later, in 1973, the United States agreed to a ceasefire in Vietnam. Between the United States and the USSR, a new era of "peaceful coexistence" began, inaugurating a new policy of cooperation known as "détente".

DOI: 10.4324/9781003533719-6

All's well that ends well, even if "history is not always as black and white as the pieces on a chessboard" (D. Johnson).

The Cold War, much like chess, was regarded as an intellectual confrontation. In the 1950s and 1960s, game theory gained prominence as a tool for understanding strategic military and economic interactions during the Cold War. Researchers used it to model and analyze conflict and cooperation between the United States and the Soviet Union.

No chapter on negotiations would be complete without discussing the prisoner's dilemma. Assuming most readers are familiar with it, we will limit the traditional prisoner's dilemma to a technical box while presenting an alternative story: the "dilemma of ordering coffee at Starbucks". This narrative is more impactful as it introduces key insights from the iterated prisoner's dilemma (IPD) as well.

The dilemma of ordering coffee at Starbucks

Consider two situations:

1 A Starbucks outlet at the London Gatwick airport.
2 A Starbucks outlet near your home.

In the first scenario, we face the classic prisoner's dilemma situation where, knowing that we and the barman will never meet again, the likely outcome tends to be mutual defection. The barman might defect by serving us a stale croissant to clear old inventory without incurring a financial loss. On our side, defection might involve giving the barman a damaged banknote to get rid of it without losing its value.

The second case, involving a Starbucks outlet near our home, is entirely different. If we visit there every morning for breakfast, mutual defection is unlikely to become an equilibrium point. If the barman tries to serve us a stale croissant or we try to pass off a damaged banknote, the other party can retaliate the next day. In repeated interactions, the potential for retaliation fosters a relationship of trust, which is far more beneficial in the long term for both parties than continuous mutual defection.

The prisoner's dilemma

After setting the stage with the dilemma of ordering coffee at Starbucks, let's turn to the traditional formulation of the prisoner's dilemma. This corresponds to our first scenario of a Starbucks outlet at London Gatwick Airport, where we previously anticipated that the equilibrium will be mutual betrayal.

The classic formulation of the prisoner's dilemma is as follows: Two criminals are accused of committing a crime. The police detain them and place them in separate cells, preventing any communication between them. Each criminal is presented with two options: confess or remain silent, under these conditions:

1. If only one confesses, the confessor avoids jail time, while the other receives a seven-year prison sentence.
2. If both confess, they each receive a six-year sentence.
3. If neither confesses, they each receive a one-year sentence.

Graphically, the prisoner's dilemma can be represented by a matrix of the gains (payoff) for each pair of decisions (as per Figure 6.1):

From an external viewpoint, it might seem rational to expect both criminals to remain silent to minimize their collective jail time. However, if one decides to stay silent with good intentions, there's a risk that the other prisoner could defect to gain full freedom, leaving the first prisoner with a seven-year sentence. This creates a similar dilemma for the other criminal: if they opt to stay silent to reduce both sentences, they risk being betrayed by the first prisoner, which would result in a seven-year sentence as a harsh consequence for their good intentions.

So what is the best strategy between confessing and staying silent, knowing that

1. If a prisoner confesses, they will get zero or six years
2. If a prisoner does not confess, they will get one or seven years

Each prisoner aims to minimize their own jail time. Given the options, it is evident that confessing guarantees a better outcome (zero or six years) compared to remaining silent (one or seven years). Consequently, both prisoners will rationally choose to confess, leading them to betray each other and get six years in jail each.

		Prisoner A	
		Confesses	**Does Not confess**
Prisoner B	**Confesses**	(6; 6)	(0; 7)
	Does Not confess	(7; 0)	(1; 1)

Figure 6.1 Prisoner's dilemma—matrix of payoffs

In technical terms, the "stay silent/cooperate" strategy is strictly dominated by the "confess/defect" strategy. Consequently, the scenario where both prisoners choose to defect is known as a Nash equilibrium.

This outcome may seem counterintuitive and paradoxical, as one might expect that two rational criminals would agree to both remain silent to minimize their combined jail time. However, achieving this would require a binding agreement enforced by an institution that monitors compliance and penalizes any violations, which is a fundamentally different type of game from the prisoner's dilemma. This scenario mirrors what occurred in the cigarette industry, where producers were locked in an equilibrium of matching each other's advertising expenditures, thereby nullifying any impact on market shares. It is thus unsurprising that cigarette companies became the strongest advocates for the ban on tobacco advertising and for having an authority to enforce compliance. This shift allowed the companies to reach a more profitable equilibrium where advertising was prohibited, maintaining the same market share distribution but without the costs of advertising campaigns.

Another paradox arising from the prisoner's dilemma involves the intrusion of randomness: if both prisoners left their decisions to chance by flipping a coin, they would likely spend less time in prison compared to the six years resulting from the Nash equilibrium "rational" choice.

With a coin flip, the expected prison time would be 3.5 years, calculated as follows: 0.25 × 7 years + 0.25 × 6 years + 0.25 × 1 year + 0.25 × 0 years, reflecting the average of the four possible outcomes. Thus, using chance seems a better option than applying logic, highlighting the paradox. However, this approach would require both players to agree to flip a coin, necessitating a binding agreement and again creating a game with different rules from the original prisoner's dilemma.

IPD: iterated prisoner's dilemma or the theoretical framework for repeated negotiations

The bitter taste left by the prisoner's dilemma's tendency toward betrayal is somewhat alleviated when the game is repeated multiple times. In this scenario, known as the IPD, humanity finds reassurance that trust and cooperation can indeed shape human relationships, aligning with common intuition and everyday experiences.

In the IPD, cooperation and trust can emerge spontaneously if the following conditions are met:

1 The number of iterations (N) is unknown
2 Twice the reward for mutual cooperation is greater than the sum of the temptation to defect and the consolation for being deceived ($2R > T + S$)

The first condition is fairly intuitive: if the negotiation is played exactly N times and both players know N, they will likely defect in the last (Nth) round to maximize their advantage, knowing the opponent cannot retaliate in the next round. This reasoning extends backward, causing both players to defect in the N – 1th round in anticipation of defection in the Nth round, and so on, all the way to the first round. Consequently, if N is known, the only possible equilibrium is mutual defection in every round. Therefore, uncertainty about the value of N is essential for establishing a relationship of mutual trust.

For the interpretation of the second condition, we can model a generic prisoner game as in Figure 6.2.

Where we have replaced the option "does not confess" with the more general "cooperates" and the option "confesses" with the more general "defects".

The letters in the quadrants indicate the gains (payoff) and stand for:

- T: **Temptation to defect**
- R: **Reward for mutual cooperation**
- P: **Punishment for mutual defection**
- S: **Sucker's payoff**

In all cases where T>R>P>S, the prisoner's dilemma will have a Nash equilibrium with both players defecting.

With the additional condition that 2R > T + S (the double reward for mutual cooperation is greater than the sum of the temptation to defect and the sucker's payoff), we can show that long-term mutual cooperation yields a greater reward than alternating between cooperation and defection. This aligns more closely with rational expectations and observed human behavior.

A surprising result is the ranking of winners in IPD tournaments among software programs that use different negotiating strategies. These strategies rely on memory of previous outcomes and algorithms that decide whether to cooperate or defect. For instance, one strategy might be to always defect regardless of the opponent's behavior, while another might

		Prisoner A	
		Cooperates	Defects
Prisoner B	Cooperates	(R;R)	(S;T)
	Defects	(T;S)	(P;P)

Figure 6.2 Prisoner's dilemma—matrix of general payoffs

involve cooperating in the first round and then mimicking the opponent's previous move.

In repeated tournaments over extended periods, involving many players and diverse negotiating strategies, hostile and greedy algorithms (which primarily exhibit defective behaviors) often perform significantly worse than altruistic algorithms (which predominantly cooperate). These tournaments demonstrate how altruistic behaviors can emerge through natural selection from mechanisms that are initially driven by pure self-interest (maximization of personal gain).

The strategy with the best performance to date is known as *Tit for Tat* and has an extremely simple structure:

- Cooperate in the first round of negotiations
- At the "n" round, replicate the opponent's strategy at the "n−1" round

The analysis of the best strategies that participated in the tournament have shown that the success of an algorithm is determined by the following characteristics:

- Goodness. The strategy must be good, in the sense that it is better not to defect before your opponent does or, inversely, to always cooperate unless provoked.
- Retaliatory. Punish the opponent's defection by defecting. Strategies that are excessively benevolent, naively optimistic, as for example "always cooperate", will be exploited mercilessly by more aggressive strategies.
- Forgiving. Forgiveness helps to re-establish a series of mutual collaborations after a series of defections, since the reward R in the case of mutual cooperation is greater than the punishment P in the event of mutual defection.
- Not jealous. It must not aim for a higher score than its opponent. Generally a "good" strategy will always lose in a direct challenge against a "mean" strategy but it will win when the scores of all the various challenges are summed up. The optimal strategy for a single prisoner's dilemma is defect, as well as for an IPD, where N is known.

To explain the success of good non-jealous strategies, let us divide the population into equal parts between strategies that "always defect" and "tit for tat" strategies.

When "always defect" strategies play against each other, they will receive P (punishment for defection) in each round. In contrast, when tit for tat strategies play against each other, they will receive R (reward for mutual cooperation) in each round, with R > P. When a tit for tat strategy plays against an "always defect" algorithm, tit for tat will suffer a marginal loss in the first round (as it will cooperate against the opponent's defection) and will then enter a cycle of mutual defections, rewarded with P for both players. By the end of the tournament, tit for tat will have accumulated (m−1)N(R+P) compared to 2(m−1)NP for the "always defect" strategy, where "m" is the number of participants, "m−1" is the number of games each participant plays, and "N" is the number of rounds in each game. Since R>P (the prisoner's dilemma assumption) one arrives at $(m-1)N(R+P) > 2\ (m-1)NP$, demonstrating that the "good" algorithm wins over the "mean" ones.

Many of Richard Dawkins' insights into the evolution of stable cooperative behavior in animals[2] are based on applying Nash equilibrium to repeated games. For instance, consider a population of organisms competing for food with two possible strategies:

- Hawks, who fight aggressively for food and only withdraw if they are severely injured.
- Pigeons, who display aggression but flee at the first serious threat to their safety.

When hawks encounter each other, there is a winner and a loser, with the loser suffering serious injuries. When pigeons confront each other, they engage in a show of aggression but ultimately back down, only wasting valuable time that could have been spent foraging but avoiding any injury. As hawks will consistently outperform pigeons, one might expect that pigeons would eventually become extinct. However, similar to the tit for tat strategy in the prisoner's dilemma, it can be shown that an equilibrium will emerge where both pigeons and hawks coexist, depending on the payoff associated with different conflict outcomes.

In this equilibrium, pigeons will continue to survive in good health.

Chess and negotiations

Negotiation theory and game theory are closely intertwined because game theory provides a structured framework to analyze strategic interactions where the outcomes of one party depend on the actions of others.

To extend De Groot's strategic thinking model to negotiations where the ultimate goal must align, at least in part, with the counterpart's objective, we can adapt the model to include a second player with their own mental schemes (see Figure 6.3). The intersection of the two players' mental schemes represents the Zone of Possible Agreement (ZOPA) the identification of the ZOPA is typically the primary goal in any negotiation.

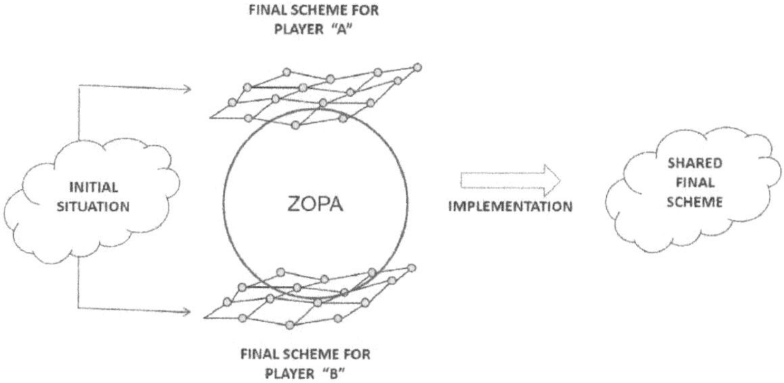

Figure 6.3 ZOPA in De Groot's strategic thinking model

When the ZOPA does not exist, we enter the realm of zero-sum negotiations, such as "fixed pie" distributive competitive negotiations. In such scenarios, one party emerges as the clear winner while the other is the loser because their interests do not overlap. The most collaborative outcome achievable is simply splitting the pie in half without negotiation.

Chess serves as a potent metaphor for zero-sum negotiations, where the fixed pie equates to a single point that can either be won exclusively by one party or split evenly in the event of a draw.

With this equivalence established, let's explore the insights that chess offers for human negotiations.

First mover's (dis)advantage

The first mover's (dis)advantage is a typical concept in asymmetrical games where players take turns making moves. It does not apply to games where players make their moves simultaneously, such as submitting sealed bids in a public tender.

We use the dual term advantage/disadvantage because making the first move does not necessarily confer an advantage. In fact, it can result in a disadvantage, often accompanied by regret for not allowing the opponent to make the first move.

The concept of the first mover's (dis)advantage in zero-sum asymmetrical negotiations is derived from chess, where it is clearly quantified through historical game statistics. In chess, the player with the white pieces, who moves first, consistently wins slightly more often than the player with the black pieces (approximately 38% versus Black's 28%, with draws making up the remaining 34%). Thus, the first mover's advantage in chess is quantified at around 10%, which is the difference between White's and Black's winning chances.

The consensus that the first mover should aim to win can be a psychological burden, leading to losses from trying too hard. In chess, some symmetrical openings, where Black's moves mirror White's, can result in White losing by attempting to force a win and prevent Black from securing a draw through repetition of moves.

The dual nature of the first mover's (dis)advantage has been highlighted and quantified not only in chess but also in business. In a Harvard Business Review article,[3] the first mover's advantage was described as a half-truth due to a lack of supporting evidence linking first mover status to success.

Examples of successful first movers include Coca-Cola and Amazon. When Coca-Cola was launched in 1886, it was one of the first fizzy drinks, though not the very first. Amazon's early entry into the e-commerce space enabled it to establish a profitable business model, shape the entire market, and build a strong brand.

The curse of being the first mover lies in the market information provided to competitors if the initial attempt fails. Competitors can learn from the first mover's mistakes and re-engineer the new product or service to ensure its success.

This is what occurred in the social media market at the beginning of this century. First movers like Friendster and Myspace failed, ultimately demonstrating to Facebook the path to success.

Stalemate

A stalemate is a common chess scenario where the player whose turn it is to move is not in check but has no legal moves available. In such cases, the game is deemed a draw, and no one wins.

Similarly, in negotiations, a stalemate can occur when neither party can gain an advantage nor is willing to make further concessions. These situations are technically referred to as deadlocks.

Unlike in chess, stalemates in business negotiations can often be resolved. Various techniques can be employed, such as taking a break from negotiations, organizing informal off-the-record meetings to explore alternative solutions, or even changing the negotiators involved.

An example of a deadlock in international negotiations is the Cuban Missile Crisis of October 1962, when the world came closest to nuclear war. The crisis began with the Soviet Union's plans to install nuclear missiles in Cuba as retaliation for the US deployment of nuclear warheads in Italy and Turkey. Initial negotiations to dissuade the Soviet Union failed, leading to a dangerous deadlock on October 22 when President Kennedy ordered a naval blockade to stop further missiles from reaching Cuba. The blockade was not recognized by the Soviets, who were prepared to reach Cuba's shores with their military fleet.

The stalemate was eventually resolved through secret, off-the-record negotiations. Kennedy agreed to dismantle the offensive weapons the US had deployed in Turkey. These secret agreements became public only 25 years later when the state secret expired. In 1962, the official agreement stipulated only that the Soviet Union would withdraw their missiles from Cuba in exchange for the US's commitment not to invade Cuba. This commitment alone would not have been enough to break the stalemate without the side secret agreements.

Minimax negotiating strategy

Pre-neural network chess software has proven that the optimal strategy to win in a zero-sum sequential negotiation is the Minimax strategy, aimed at minimizing the opponent's maximum advantage by limiting their best options—a significant departure from the more instinctive negotiation strategy of bolstering one's own strengths. Game theory pioneers such as John von Neumann and Emil Borel are credited with introducing the Minimax algorithm.

For mathematics enthusiasts, it can be said that in two-player zero-sum games, the Minimax solution is equivalent to the Nash equilibrium. This is a scenario where no player can benefit by altering their strategy unilaterally.

Let's exemplify this algorithm with a practical scenario: selling a house. The Minimax strategy proposes that instead of enhancing the house's strengths before negotiating with potential buyers, the focus should be on mitigating the buyer's best alternatives to negotiate a lower price. This involves preparing solid justifications to minimize any shortcomings of the house.

Zeitnot

In chess with time control, the German term "zeitnot" describes a situation where a player has very little time remaining to make their moves. Under time pressure, players tend to move faster and have less time to think, which increases the likelihood of making mistakes.

In negotiations, "zeitnot" is used to constrain the time available for the opponent to make a decision. For example, in parliamentary discussions, the government might bring up an issue just before a looming deadline to prevent the opposition from organizing effectively to block the decision.

Anchoring

Anchoring in a negotiation refers to the initial price or offer made by either party, which subconsciously influences the negotiation process.

Both parties may find it difficult to deviate from this initial value, even if conditions change. As discussed in the chapter on decision-making, anchoring is a cognitive bias, first demonstrated by Kahneman in studies where participants were requested to estimate the percentage of African nations in the UN. Those asked if the percentage was "more or less than 10%" tended to give lower estimates (averaging 25%), while those asked if it was "more or less than 65%" provided higher estimates (averaging 45%).[4]

In chess, this bias manifests more subtly. For instance, a player who starts with an aggressive and tactical opening might maintain an aggressive approach throughout the game, even if the position evolves into a simplified and balanced endgame. However, chess players learn from wins and losses, how to adjust their strategies based on an objective assessment of the position.

In contrast, managers lack frequent opportunities to refine their negotiation skills through practice, as business negotiations tend to occur occasionally.

Negotiation process

Negotiation, much like chess, is an art that requires astuteness, intelligence, patience, expertise, and discipline to navigate circumstances toward the most advantageous position. In both fields, the process begins with thorough preparation, gathering comprehensive information about the opponent. With adequate preparation, a favorable outcome can often be secured even before the negotiation begins. This occurs when the preparation phase successfully identifies a ZOPA, allowing us to formulate an offer within that range. As a result, we can present an offer at the negotiation table that is likely to be immediately accepted by the other party.

Similarly, in chess, strategic victories can be set up before the game begins. Many players have experienced instances where detailed preparatory studies revealed subtle weaknesses in their opponent's style, which were then exploited during the match under the right circumstances.

After the preparatory phase, a game of chess unfolds in three stages: the opening, middle game, and endgame, each reflecting the phases of a negotiation. In the opening, players establish their style and lay the groundwork for the negotiation. For example, initiating with a king's pawn opening (1.e4) is akin to setting a strategic anchor around a specific dynamic, such as fully or partially open gameplay.

The progression of the game mirrors the dynamics of negotiations: those with an advantage aim to ease tensions, while those at a disadvantage introduce complexities, launch new offensives, and present fresh arguments (Figure 6.4).

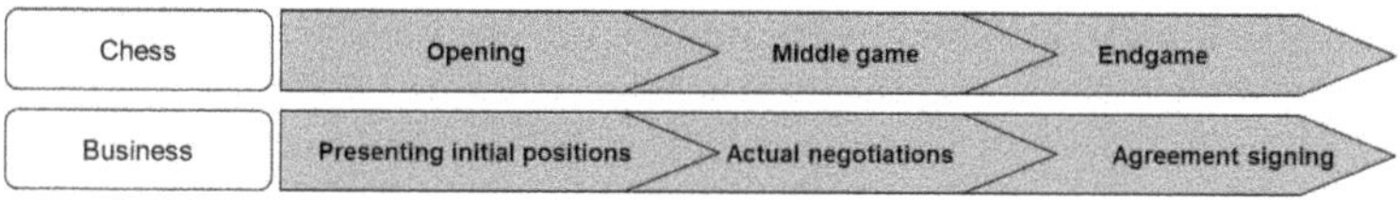

Figure 6.4 Phases in chess and in negotiations

Just as the opening moves influence the progression of the game, the conclusion must also be carefully considered: checkmate in chess or the signing of a contract at the end of a negotiation. There is an optimal moment to conclude both the game and the negotiation. Hesitation at this crucial time poses a potential risk, introducing elements that could jeopardize the victory. Conversely, it is important not to rush the conclusion prematurely. Attempting to checkmate the opponent's King too hastily in chess or prematurely concluding negotiations may undermine an almost certain positive outcome. Therefore, hesitation or rushing at the end of a chess game or a negotiation are the primary risks that can nullify all the efforts made during the preparatory phase and the negotiation process.

If a series of negotiations or chess games conclude successfully, there is a risk of becoming complacent (which is why sales agents are often rotated). Success can lead to a lack of motivation or, as Kasparov puts it, "success is the enemy of future success".

Impossible negotiations

An impossible negotiation is defined as one that is doomed to fail from the start. However, even in such cases, it can still be worthwhile to engage in the negotiation process.

Playing chess against a world champion

Imagine that you are a chess amateur and you have to play a game against former world champion Anatoly Karpov. You know from the start that you are going to lose. A draw is the best result you can hope for if Karpov is playing simultaneously against you and 30 other amateurs. In the days leading up to the game, you cancel all interactions with friends, family, and colleagues to deeply study the opening you'll play for this important occasion. When the day arrives, you make no obvious mistakes in the opening phase and feel proud to demonstrate a decent knowledge of the game in front of one of the chess legends. However, as the game progresses, you gradually realize that you have slowly but steadily slipped into an inferior position, without fully understanding how it happened. While defeat isn't imminent, you still desperately cling to the possibility of securing a draw. However, with each subsequent move, the unease intensifies until the moment you reluctantly resign to avoid an embarrassing checkmate, which is just a few moves away.

Following this painful but anticipated defeat, you once again isolate yourself, meticulously analyzing each move from the game. This thorough examination, coupled with your preparatory analysis, positions you as an expert in that particular opening and middle game within your local chess club. Consequently, what initially appeared to be an insurmountable challenge transforms into one of the most valuable learning experiences of your chess journey.

Playing against death

Is there a lesson to be learned from an impossible negotiation with death? In Ingmar Bergman's 1957 film "The Seventh Seal", Antonius Block, a knight returning from the Crusades to a plague-ridden Sweden, confronts death on a deserted beach. Antonius challenges death to a game of chess, aiming to postpone his unavoidable destiny and utilize the additional time for contemplation of existential questions.

Antonius negotiates with death through a game of chess. But what is the point of this negotiation if the outcome is known in advance? If Antonius knew for certain that he would be checkmated in two moves, he would likely have surrendered immediately, without even issuing the challenge. Any resistance would have been futile. However, the uncertainty surrounding the number of moves N made accepting the challenge worthwhile. In mathematical terms, we are dealing with a repeated negotiation with an unknown N (see paragraph on IPD).

Although life is destined for an inevitable end, it is worth living because of the uncertainty surrounding the final moment. If I knew I would die tomorrow, I might choose to end my life today. However, if I were willing to end my life today, I might have done it yesterday instead. This backward induction process leads us back to the day of our birth, making life seem unworthy of living.

Living becomes impossible if we know we will die on a specific day. Paradoxically, what makes life worth living is knowing that we will die, but not knowing when.

Playing against two world champions

Alright, let's increase the impossibility of the initial challenge twofold. Now, you'll be playing against not just one but two former world champions: Anatoly Karpov with the Black pieces and Garry Kasparov with the White pieces. The goal is to achieve at least one point, whether through a win or two draws.

The method is exceptionally refined and was utilized by the English illusionist Derren Brown, who knows nothing about chess. He successfully earned four points in eight simultaneous games against eight chess masters. This technique is unrelated to hypnosis, which is Derren Brown's area of expertise. The technique involves mirroring the moves of each champion on the other chessboard, effectively setting them up to compete directly against each other. Figure 6.5 shows the example of the first move.[5]

Having learned to manage two simultaneous games against Karpov and Kasparov, we will now explore a financial application of the mirroring technique, commonly referred to as internal hedging in business contexts.

Let's imagine your European company receives a monthly payment in dollars from an American client. Every month, you must convert these dollars through a bank, incurring fees and being exposed to fluctuating euro-dollar exchange rates.

Additionally, if you need to pay for raw materials, some invoices, like those for oil, might be denominated in dollars. This means you have to convert euros into dollars to settle these bills, again incurring fees and facing the risk of exchange rate fluctuations.

To tackle these challenges effectively, you can reduce the risks associated with the two euro-dollar transactions by avoiding double bank fees and minimizing exposure to fluctuations in the euro-dollar exchange rate. The solution, known as internal hedging, involves opening a dollar-denominated bank account. This allows you to pay your supplier directly in dollars using the funds received from your American client.

A touch of magic is always welcome, whether in finance or in chess.

Conclusions

Chess is often seen as an inadequate analogy for real negotiations because of its zero-sum nature, which contrasts with more desirable win-win approaches. Be cautious: as in a prisoner's dilemma, if you approach a negotiation with a win-win mindset and face an opponent using a win-lose strategy, who do you think will win the negotiation?

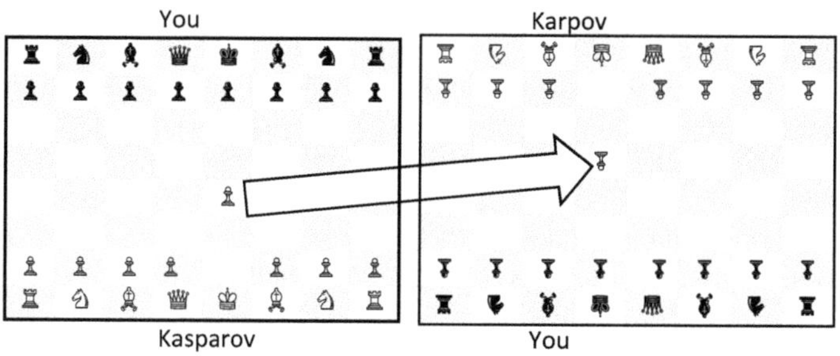

Figure 6.5 Playing against two world champions

Chapter 6—Negotiations—interviews

Luca Desiata interviewed by Bachar Kouatly

What types of negotiations have you experienced in your professional life?

Having participated in numerous M&A transactions in the energy sector, most of my experience involves zero-sum negotiations. In these cases, the premium or discount set for the transaction price benefits only one party, resulting in an advantage or disadvantage for just one side.

Can you provide an example of a win-win negotiation you have been involved in?

In 2009, as Head of Nuclear Development for the Italian multinational electricity producer, I led the negotiations for the Shareholders' Agreement with the French nuclear technology partner for the construction of four nuclear plants in Italy, a project valued at over 20 billion euros. In this case, the project's cost was not a primary issue in the negotiations, as budget overruns during construction had proven to be more significant than the initial price. The main focus was on maximizing industrial development and GDP growth for Italy and France, whose Prime Ministers, Sarkozy and Berlusconi, had signed a nuclear cooperation agreement two years earlier.

The negotiation process was highly collaborative, with both teams concentrating on the long-term benefits of the project. Unfortunately, the initiative was abruptly halted following the Fukushima nuclear disaster and the subsequent anti-nuclear referendum in June 2011.

Can you share an example of an unusual or entertaining negotiation you've participated in?

The most unusual and entertaining negotiation I was involved in concerned the sale of a 1% share of my start-up, pptArt, the world's first art crowdsourcing platform. The challenge in valuing a newly incorporated start-up stemmed from the absence of historical financial data and the lack of comparable companies in the highly innovative sector. These factors rendered traditional valuation methods, such as discounted cash flow (DCF), multiples, or Payback Time, ineffective. All the investors I spoke with considered relying solely on forecast P&L to be too risky.

As a result, the negotiation process degenerated into rather unprofessional haggling. To move beyond these clandestine and personal negotiations, I decided to organize an auction at an art house in Rome, treating the company's investment memo as if it were a work of art. This approach aimed to reveal the highest value investors were prepared to offer for such an innovative concept as art crowdsourcing. In the days leading up to the auction, I received an irresistible offer that valued the start-up at €3 million. Consequently, I chose to cancel the auction and accept the offer.

Introduction

Following the epic showdown between Russian champion Boris Spassky and American challenger Bobby Fischer, the only other chess World Championship to capture global attention was the 1984 match between the reigning champion Anatoly Karpov and the young challenger Garry Kasparov. This championship lasted five months and featured 48 games, yet it was still inconclusive. After Karpov took a 4-0 lead in the first nine games, the match settled into a long series of draws, interrupted only by Karpov's fifth victory. With the score at 5-0 in favor of Karpov, the challenger seemed to have little chance. However, in the 32nd game, Kasparov staged a dramatic comeback, winning three games, including two consecutively, and bringing the score to 5-3.

After five months of intense stress, both players' health had deteriorated significantly, with Karpov, in particular, losing over 10 kg. FIDE President Florencio Campomanes intervened and halted the championship without the players' consent. The World Championship was then rescheduled for 1985, reverting to a 24-game format, which was won by Kasparov. In accordance with an agreement made prior to the 1985 World Championship, another match was held in 1986 to compensate Karpov for the interruption of the 1984 match, where he had held a 5-3 lead over Kasparov.

Kasparov successfully defended his title in 1986. The two players, Karpov and Kasparov, fought for the World Championship twice more, in 1987 and 1990. The 1987 match ended in a tie (12-12), which enabled Kasparov to keep his title.

Here is a summary of the 5 K-K world championships:

- 1984 Moscow: Karpov-Kasparov 25-23, championship stopped and canceled
- 1985 Moscow: Kasparov-Karpov 13-11, Kasparov wins the title of world champion
- 1986 London-Leningrad: Kasparov-Karpov 12.5-11.5
- 1987 Seville: Kasparov-Karpov 12-12. Kasparov, as the incumbent champion, retains the title
- 1990 New York, Lyon: Kasparov-Karpov 12.5-11.5

Anatoly Karpov interviewed by Bachar Kouatly

Anatoly, in the first match against Kasparov in 1984, you were leading 5-0 up to the 31st game. What happened after?

It is not so easy to identify a single factor to explain the turnaround from 5-0 to 5-3.

The beginning of the tournament was exceptionally favorable for me. I recall winning four of the first nine games quickly. After that, I had 17 draws, but then I secured another victory, taking a clear lead with a score of 5-0.

At that point, I had a strong chance to win 6-0, so I was waiting for the right moment to secure a shutout. Unfortunately, in the 31st game, I missed a significant opportunity to win both during the middle game and after the 40th move. This led to a loss in the 32nd game, as I was still reeling from the missed chance in the previous game. There's a saying that "if you don't take advantage of a clear opportunity, you risk letting your opponent make a comeback".

With my goal of a 6-0 victory now out of reach, I experienced some demotivation.

Meanwhile, Kasparov had completely recovered from the initial shock of his five defeats. With nothing left to lose and energized by his victory in the 32nd game, he started playing with renewed precision and consistency, displaying his aggressive style more effectively. In the 41st game, I missed a second opportunity to close out the championship, as I reached a position where I could have secured a win. I saw the winning combination but I was in zeitnot[6] and could not calculate all the possible alternatives. Fearing that I might lose control, I opted for a cautious continuation, which unfortunately only resulted in a draw.

A lengthy series of draws ensued. Today, after many years, this extended sequence has been recast in public memory as an epic struggle between titans. At the time, however, it was seen as frustrating for the organizers and rather dull for the audience.

After the first 30 games, external forces began to disrupt the normal flow of the match, affecting our ability to stay focused and maintain high standards of play. Naturally, such interferences tend to benefit the player at a disadvantage, who stands to gain from any change in conditions. Our match was no exception to this rule.

Could you provide some comments on the conclusion, or more accurately, on the interruption of the first match?

After 45 days of play and 48 games, including 40 draws, it was clear that an easy resolution was unlikely. Everyone—players, spectators, and organizers—was exhausted. Fédération Internationale Des Échecs (FIDE) decided to suspend the championship and reorganize it with new rules, notably including a limit on the number of games.

At the time of the interruption, FIDE justified the decision by citing the deteriorating health of the players. However, the true reason behind the decision was that all high-level chess events had come to a standstill: the new round of the candidates' tournament had been postponed, the press had lost interest in our championship, and even the Soviet government was embarrassed by the extended duration of the match, which had kept the Hall of Columns at the Trade Union House[7] occupied for so long. This venue was an important government building, where other events had already been scheduled (including Ustinov's[8] state funeral that imposed a temporary break during our 1984 match). Additionally, Chernenko[9] was in a state of clinical death, and it was anticipated that the Hall of Columns would soon be required for a major state funeral lasting at least a week. As a result, we were moved to a hotel where the playing conditions and levels of concentration were significantly compromised. This further altered the dynamics in Kasparov's favor. By the time the match was interrupted, he had improved his score to 5-3.

What was your opinion about this suspension?

I was strongly opposed to the interruption but had to comply due to intense political pressure. Despite Kasparov's resurgence and the challenging circumstances, I still held a significant 2-point lead and was confident in my ability to win. Political and organizational controversies were escalating. I was seen as a long-standing figure in the Russian political establishment, making me more acceptable to the current Soviet government. In contrast, Kasparov, who had only recently joined the Komsomol[10], was viewed as young, restless, and somewhat rebellious. However, it's important to note that Kasparov had the support of his compatriot, Aleyev, who would later become the President of Azerbaijan and run against Gorbachev to replace Chernenko. Aleyev played a crucial role with the Sports Ministry in suspending the tournament to benefit his protégé.

In conclusion, at the time of the suspension, I was leading the match and thus was the most adversely affected.

From a chess perspective, what was your novelty that most impressed Kasparov?

I prefer discussing new approaches and strategies rather than focusing on individual moves. A novel move is always part of a broader plan, and as noted in the chapter on strategic thinking, human players can't conceive a move outside of a plan.

I think I impressed Kasparov with my approach to the Tarrasch variation in the Queen's Gambit while playing White. After suffering two losses against this opening, Kasparov abandoned it not just against me but also against other opponents.

Another significant achievement was my handling of Kasparov's Grünfeld Defense. Notably, my move 17. Qa4 (Queen to a4) in Belfort in 1988, which aimed to weaken Black's position, stands out.

Additionally, in the ninth game of our second match in Moscow in 1984, I made a memorable pawn sacrifice with 47. Ng2 (Knight to g2) in the endgame. This sacrifice is considered one of the finest in chess history. Kasparov was so taken aback that he couldn't find the right continuation and ultimately lost the game.

On Kasparov's part, he made significant contributions to the Spanish Game with numerous innovative attacking ideas and revitalized the King's Indian Defense, which had previously been less popular.

Overall, our extended rivalry made a remarkable contribution to chess history. It was also one of the last world championships where computers were not heavily used for preparation, marking it as one of the last truly human, passionate, and intense battles.

An overall assessment of your challenges against Kasparov?

Overall, we competed in 144 games across five world championships. I won 19 of these games, Kasparov 21, while the remaining 104 ended in draws. This reflects a significant level of parity, where the final outcome was largely influenced by the rules and tournament organization, as well as the psychological and fatigue factors.

I see myself as a player with a universal style, striving for beauty, consistency, and perfection in every game, regardless of external conditions or opponents.

In contrast, Kasparov thrives on a more personal approach, often needing to channel a strong animosity toward his opponent to play at his best. His dynamic style is reminiscent of Botvinnik and Korchnoi.

In summary, beyond the specific events and circumstances, our rivalry will be remembered as the last great human clash in chess before computers began to reshape the game and the personalities of its champions.

Notes

1 https://www.telegraph.co.uk/culture/books/non_fictionreviews/3669446/How-Bobby-Fischer-and-Boris-Spassky-became-pawns.html.
2 R. Dawkins. *The Selfish Gene* (Oxford, 1976).
3 https://hbr.org/2005/04/the-half-truth-of-first-mover-advantage.
4 A. Tversky, & D. Kahneman. "Judgment under Uncertainty: Heuristics and Biases", *Science*, New Series, Vol. 185 (1974).
5 Both chessboards are drawn using Unicode chess pieces by piliapp.com.
6 Time trouble.
7 the venue where Karpov had been crowned world champion ten years earlier.
8 Defense Minister.
9 General Secretary of the Communist Party of the Soviet Union.
10 Komsomol: ***Kom****munističeskij* **So***juz* **Mol***odëži* , was the youth organization of the Communist Party of the Soviet Unions.

Chapter 7

Leadership

Want to Improve Your Leadership Skills? Play Chess!

This was the title of a 2014 article by Samuel Hunt, a Professor at Western Kentucky University, and Joseph Cangemi.[1]

To support their claim, the authors point out that many of the world's billionaires, including Georges Soros, Bill Gates, Larry Ellison, and Peter Thiel, are avid chess players.

Leadership model

As anticipated in the introduction chapter of this book, leadership is the key ingredient that binds strategy formulation and strategy execution together in order to achieve success.

Discussing leadership in the context of chess might seem unusual at first, as chess is fundamentally a solitary and introspective activity, whereas corporate leadership generally involves directing a team toward common goals.

However, this analogy becomes particularly relevant when we focus on the leader's personal attributes and inherent qualities, particularly their strategic acumen.

Prominent figures in the chess world have often been acknowledged for their leadership qualities. For example, Magnus Carlsen, the young Norwegian world champion ranked number one globally by ELO, was listed among Time magazine's 100 most influential people in the world in 2013. Similarly, former world champion Garry Kasparov made the same list in 2007, not solely for his chess accomplishments (he had retired in 2005) but for his political stance against Vladimir Putin.

Chess has long symbolized the triumph of talent and intelligence over chance and unpredictability. Since the Middle Ages, it has been linked with morality, notably when the second most widely distributed book after the Bible was the Dominican monk Jacopo da Cessole's treatise "Liber de moribus hominum et officiis nobilium super ludo scacchorum"

DOI: 10.4324/9781003533719-7

or "The Customs of Men and the Duties of Nobles". This text used chess to depict social dynamics, assigning each pawn a specific social role (farmer, blacksmith, tailor, merchant, etc.) and deriving human duties from the rules and visual aspects of chess pieces. A chess game thus became a parable, illustrating the moral values of real-life scenarios.

In the Enlightenment era, chess evolved into a symbol of meritocracy, where success was seen as a reward for skill and talent rather than wealth, luck, or social privilege.

The celebration of chess persisted across various eras and regions.

Chess celebrations: Benjamin Franklin, Napoleon, Winston Churchill, Fidel Castro, etc.

In his 1779 essay "The Morals of Chess", Benjamin Franklin wrote that[2]:

> The game of chess is not merely an idle amusement. Several very valuable qualities of the mind, useful in the course of human life, are to be acquired or strengthened by it, so as to become habits ready on all occasions; for life is a kind of chess metaphor, in which we have often points to gain and competitors or adversaries to contend with, and in which there is a vast variety of good and ill events, that are, in some degree, the effect of prudence, or the want of it.

Both Napoleon Bonaparte and Winston Churchill were avid chess players. They reportedly played matches against their generals and used chess as a tool for strategic planning and as a way to relax.

The philosopher Søren Kierkegaard compared the strategic depth of chess to the philosophical and existential complexities of life. He is known for the enigmatic quote: "I feel as if I were a piece in a game of chess, when my opponent says of it: That piece cannot be moved".

The Cuban revolutionary leader and politician Fidel Castro was also a chess enthusiast. He supported the development of chess in Cuba and believed in its educational and strategic benefits.

In the USSR, chess symbolized revolutionary ideals due to its logical and strategic nature. Soviet leaders believed that by instilling these traits in the population, they could develop stronger citizens who embodied the values of the revolution. Lenin made chess education mandatory in schools, established state-sponsored chess training programs, organized tournaments, and promoted the game as a symbol of Soviet superiority.

Enrique Peña Nieto, who served as Mexico's President from 2012 to 2018, attributed his political achievements to his proficiency in chess.

More recently, American chess champion Susan Polgar stated that "Chess is a miniature version of life. To succeed, you must be disciplined, assess your resources accurately, make responsible choices, and adapt your decisions when circumstances change".

Even more recently, the President-elect of Mexico, Enrique Peña Nieto, has credited his success to his Chess playing ability

Women and leadership

Though chess is often regarded as one of the most chauvinistic environments in modern society, it provides compelling examples of women's equal capability in leadership.

First, the Queen piece stands as an enduring testament to the significant leadership roles held by female political figures throughout history. Originally a weak piece that could only move one step diagonally, it evolved into the most powerful piece by the 15th century, influenced by the prestige of Queen Isabella of Castile. Her accomplishments, such as expelling the Moors from Spain and sponsoring Christopher Columbus, played a significant role in the transformation of the Queen piece. Other influential and charismatic female leaders of that time, including Catherine of Aragon, Elizabeth I, Mary Stuart, and Catherine de Medici, further contributed to the evolution of the chess Queen.

An even more compelling example of women's equal capability in leadership can be found in the fascinating lives of the Polgar sisters.

Laszlo Polgar was not a man to tread the beaten path. A Hungarian educational psychologist with a passion for the extraordinary, he harbored a grand ambition: to prove that geniuses are made, not born, in line with the conclusions of De Groot's studies. In the early 1960s, while most men his age were settling into conventional lives, Laszlo embarked on a unique quest. He wrote letters to women across Europe, outlining a bold project that would shape the course of his life—and the lives of his future children. In these letters, he expressed his intention to find a partner for an extraordinary experiment: to raise children who, through intense training and education, would showcase the boundless potential of the human mind.

Laszlo's vision was clear: if raised in a structured environment, any child could achieve greatness in a chosen field. He eventually found a kindred spirit in Klara, a teacher who shared his fervor for education and excellence. They married, united by a common dream to transform their future offspring into prodigies.

For their experiment, they selected chess over mathematics, music, and foreign languages because "the evaluation system in chess is more defined, established, and thus more objective and precise. This makes it easier to demonstrate the success or failure of the experiment" and "in the end, we decided that chess in itself is a complex, very valuable, and beautiful activity: a game, a science, an art, a sport, and a psychology simultaneously".[3]

In the quiet of their modest Budapest apartment, Laszlo and Klara set to work, long before their children were even born. They filled their home with books, chessboards, and educational toys. They researched methods and strategies, preparing meticulously for the arrival of their future champions.

On April 19, 1969, their first daughter, Susan, was born. From the moment she could sit up, Laszlo began teaching her chess, believing it to be the perfect tool to cultivate intellectual rigor. Susan's tiny hands moved the chess pieces across the board, guided by her father's patient instructions. By the age of four, she was competing in local tournaments, her eyes gleaming with the thrill of the game.

The Polgar home buzzed with activity, an educational laboratory brimming with energy and ambition. Sophia, born in 1974, and Judith, born in 1976, joined the family, each child seamlessly entering the rigorous regime Laszlo had devised. The sisters were surrounded by books and chessboards, their days structured around learning and practice.

However, when the Polgar sisters were born, the chess world was a bastion of male dominance, with deeply entrenched biases and structural barriers that made it challenging for women to excel. Laszlo Polgar, with his radical educational experiment, faced numerous organizational difficulties as he endeavored to propel his daughters into the highest echelons of the chess world. Laszlo sought to enroll them in tournaments to gain experience and exposure. However, finding competitions that would accept young girls, especially in a predominantly male environment, was challenging. Many prestigious chess clubs and tournaments were reluctant to admit female players, particularly young ones. This resistance was not just from fellow competitors but also from organizers who doubted the seriousness and capability of female participants.

In addition to resistance from chess tournament organizers, Laszlo's experiment also faced skepticism and criticism from the educational community. "Children need to play" naysayers insisted. "This regimen is too harsh". But Laszlo and Klara stood firm, confident in their unconventional approach. They saw their daughters not as subjects of an experiment, but as individuals blossoming under a philosophy of excellence and perseverance.

Susan, Sophia, and Judith thrived, their childhoods intertwined with the rhythms of the chessboard. Susan, the eldest, became a Grandmaster, a title that catapulted her to international fame. Sophia, with her sharp mind and competitive spirit, followed closely, earning accolades and championships. Judith, the youngest and perhaps the most prodigious, shattered records, becoming the first woman to break into the absolute top ten of the world's chess rankings, an unprecedented achievement that stunned the world.

The Polgar sisters' story spread like wildfire, inspiring awe and admiration. There were three sisters, raised in an ordinary Budapest apartment, who had ascended to the pinnacle of the chess world. Their success was a testament to their father's vision and their own relentless dedication.

Laszlo's project, once a radical experiment, now stood as a testament to the power of nurture. The Polgar sisters had not only achieved greatness but had also demonstrated that with the right environment, guidance, and unwavering support, the boundaries of human potential could indeed be pushed to extraordinary heights. The world watched in wonder, as the Polgar family proved that genius, far from being a mere accident of birth, could be carefully, lovingly cultivated.

The association between Chess and genius: from the Romantic era to the supercomputer age

While the Polgar experiment strongly supports the influence of environmental factors, chess has historically been regarded as a game for geniuses. Let's explore some anecdotes in chess history that illustrate the association with the concept of genius.

Here is how Magnus Carlsen, the young world chess champion from Norway who has held the top spot in the world rankings since 2012, responded to a journalist a few years ago[4]:

Journalist: "What would be the opening words you would like to see in your biography?"
Carlsen: "I am not a genius"
Journalist: "And the title of the biography?"
Carlsen: "Carlsen, the chess genius"

Chess, along with music and mathematics, is often linked to the concept of genius that emerges early in life. A child prodigy might excel in playing the piano, solving complex calculations, or mastering chess from a young age—precocity being a defining trait of genius. In the 1920s, Samuel Reshevsky's parents capitalized on their son's exceptional talent when he was only 8 years old. These talents allowed him to defeat seasoned players and chess masters even in simultaneous games. His touring exhibitions ceased when American authorities intervened, accusing his parents of exploiting child labor and compelling them to enroll young Samuel in school.

The allure of genius to ordinary people partly stems from the mysterious aura surrounding its origins, as if these qualities emanated from a realm beyond our own. If everything were reducible to a mechanical formula, this fascination would instantly dissipate.

Media spectacles and sensational games such as blindfold exhibitions (where champions move pieces while blindfolded, communicating through Cartesian coordinates) or simultaneous games (where a champion competes against hundreds, moving from board to board) have undoubtedly reinforced the association between chess and superior intelligence. More recently, the astonishing advancements in science and artificial intelligence have transformed the concept of chess genius into a superhuman capable of challenging computers in analyzing thousands of variations.

In the early 19th century, the Romantic era not only revolutionized literature and the arts but also transformed chess into a symbol of unrestrained creativity and genius. During this period, chess was seen as an intellectual pursuit that transcended mere strategic play; it was an art form that celebrated brilliant, imaginative moves. The concept of the chess genius was epitomized by figures like **Paul Morphy**, a prodigy from New Orleans whose short but dazzling career left an indelible mark on the game. Morphy's exceptional skill and creativity were showcased during his European tour in 1858–1859, where he defeated many of the best players of his time. However, his sudden withdrawal from chess and subsequent personal struggles highlighted the intense, often fleeting nature of genius.

The mid-20th century marked the dominance of the Soviet School of Chess, where systematic training and scientific approaches were emphasized. Yet, prodigies continued to emerge, underscoring the persistent link between chess and genius. **Bobby Fischer**, an American prodigy, became an international sensation by winning the World Championship in 1972. Fischer's deep understanding of the game, combined with his unorthodox methods and intense drive, reaffirmed the notion that genius was critical for success in chess. His life, marked by both brilliance and controversy, further cemented the image of the chess genius as a complex, multifaceted figure. Later in life, Fischer faced legal troubles, wanted by the FBI for violating embargoes during the conflict in former Yugoslavia.

In 1920, **Samuel Reshevsky**, a Polish-born American prodigy, stunned the chess world with his abilities from a very young age. By the age of eight, Reshevsky was already defeating seasoned players and giving simultaneous exhibitions, embodying the archetype of the chess genius.

José Raúl Capablanca, a Cuban prodigy who became a World Champion in 1921, exemplified the merging of natural talent with deep strategic understanding. Capablanca's nearly effortless style and early mastery of chess basics reinforced the notion that genius was integral to achieving greatness in chess.

The advent of supercomputers in the late 20th century revolutionized chess analysis and training, yet the association with genius persisted. **Garry Kasparov**, who became the youngest World Champion in 1985, leveraged both his extraordinary intellect and the emerging power of computer analysis to dominate the chess world. Kasparov's matches against IBM's Deep Blue in the 1990s symbolized the intersection of human genius and artificial intelligence, raising questions about the future of human creativity in strategy games.

All these examples illustrate how the concept of genius in chess has evolved and adapted to the unique historical conditions of each era.

The association between youth and genius is common in intellectual activities such as music, mathematics, and chess. In technical terms, the ideal or sensitive age for starting practice in a given domain is called the "critical period". This critical period is considered the third ingredient in explaining expert performance, alongside innate abilities and practice. Some frameworks recognize that certain skills can be acquired effortlessly only during a specific early period in life, possibly due to neuroplasticity and brain development, e.g. languages. In chess, Electroencephalography (EEG) studies of players playing blindfolded have shown intense activity in the right hemisphere of the brain, confirming some form of correlation with neurophysiology.

Regarding domain-specific practice, it has been observed that becoming a chess expert requires between 1,000 and 5,000 hours of study and practice, and achieving Grandmaster status demands ten times that amount, or approximately ten years. Proponents of the "practice" factor highlight that historically acclaimed young geniuses like Bobby Fischer and Judith Polgar had spent at least ten full years practicing and studying the game before reaching fame. Comparative studies suggest that the younger a player starts studying chess, the more hours they dedicate to it, indicating a correlation between early start and amount of practice.

Ultimately, one's perception of a chess genius will depend on the examples that have left the most significant impression. For instance, witnessing 8-year-old Samuel Reshevsky simultaneously defeat 30 masters might lead one to believe in the innate nature of genius, inspired by such an extraordinary feat. Conversely, meeting one of the Polgar sisters might lead us to acknowledge the importance of practice and perseverance.

Drawing a parallel between chess and corporate leadership, it takes around ten years of intense study and practice to become a chess Grandmaster. Similarly, some studies[5] have shown that it takes an average of 24 years to become a CEO. However, there are individuals known as "sprinter CEOs" who achieve this role even faster.

This study revealed that sprinters don't reach the top by acquiring perfect pedigrees, such as MBAs from Ivy League schools or exceptional performance records at their companies. Instead, they ascend by making bold career moves that propel them to the top.

Evolution of leadership models

The leadership theory focused on personality traits seeks to pinpoint the characteristics that distinguish leaders from others. By identifying these traits, organizations can better select, train, and develop future leaders. In 2002, Judge emphasized that the "Big Five personality traits"[6] (detailed below) showed a strong correlation with leadership. He recommended selecting future leaders based on these traits.

The personality-traits leadership model originated from Carlyle's "great man" theory,[7] which posits that the course of history is shaped by the leadership of exceptional individuals.

In the second half of the 20th century, leadership theory primarily focused on analyzing the specific circumstances and contexts that give rise to leaders. Individuals who excel as leaders in one situation may not necessarily do so in others.

Only recently have these two approaches—personality and circumstances—been integrated to surpass the inherent limitations of each when considered independently. This integration involves evaluating various types of leadership personalities within the specific contexts where they have proven effective.

Among the leadership models applied in the business world, the most popular ones are the following: the Myers-Briggs Type Indicator, Cattell's 16 Personality Factors (or 16PF), and the Big-Five Personality Traits.

Most personality models are based on the "lexical hypothesis". This hypothesis posits the identification of a reservoir of personality indicators in spoken language, under the premise that "the most important personality traits in people's social lives will be encoded by words in language, such as enthusiastic, proactive, etc. The more important a trait is, the more likely it is to be expressed by a single word".

Building on this principle, in 1936 American psychologists Gordon Allport and Henry S. Odbert compiled 400,000 personality-descriptive words from Webster's New International Dictionary.[8] From this list, they extracted a subset of 4,500 words related to permanent and observable traits (see Figure 7.1).

In 1946, British psychologist Raymond Cattell built upon the work of Allport and Odbert by creating the 16PF© model.[9] He conducted a semantic analysis and synthesis of the 4,500 words, initially reducing them to 35 and then to 12 through factor analysis, which revealed correlations among them. The addition of four self-assessment factors brought the total to 16.

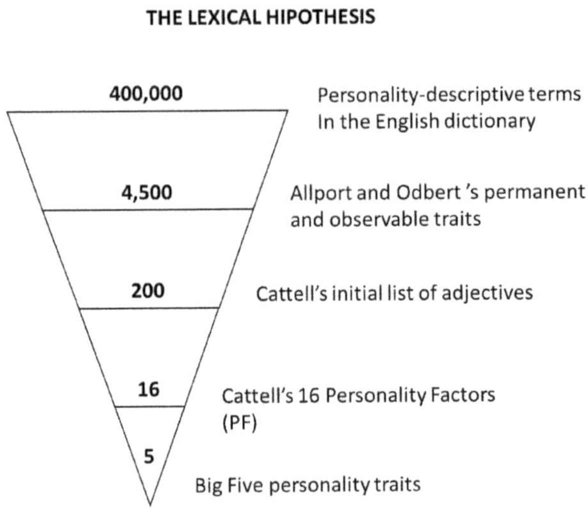

Figure 7.1 The lexical hypothesis

In 1981, Goldberg further refined these 16 traits into 5 personality descriptive factors known as the "Big Five": extraversion, agreeableness, conscientiousness, emotional stability, and openness to experience.

The Myers-Briggs indicator

In the context of the analysis of personality, the Myers-Briggs (MBTI)[10] indicator is a psychometric questionnaire that measures the psychological preferences of how people perceive the world and how they make decisions. These preferences were extrapolated from Jung's typological theories and reprocessed by Katharine Cook Briggs and her daughter Isabel Briggs Myers in 1962. Jung had proposed the existence of two pairs of bipolar cognitive functions:

- The rational functions (judgment): thinking and feeling
- The irrational functions (perception): sensation and intuition

Individuals are born, or develop, some preferred ways of thinking or acting. The MBTI ranks some of these differences in 4 opposite psychological pairs, or dichotomies (represented in Box 7.1), with 16 resulting psychological types. None of these types are better or worse. Each individual has a preference for a certain combination, similarly to those who are used to writing with the right hand or with the left.

Box 7.1 MBTI dichotomies

MBTI dichotomies

Extraversion (E)–(I) Introversion
Sensing (S)–(N) Intuition
Thinking (T)–(F) Feeling
Judging (J)–(P) Perceiving

The 16 types are identified by 4 letter initials, in which each letter represents the initial in English of the various preferences (with the exception of intuition, for which the letter N is used to avoid confusion with introversion), for example:

- ESTJ: extraversion (E), sensing (S), thinking (T), judging (J)
- IFNB: introversion (I), intuition (N), hear (F), perceiving (P)

And so on for the 16 possible combinations.

Some researchers have criticized this tool because of its low reliability: their statistical studies show that between 39% and 76% of people who have taken the test, fall into a different type when they take the test again a few weeks or months after. In addition, at the request to indicate an MBTI type in a self-evaluation, only 50% chose the same profile as the test results. Other scholars have emphasized poor evidence of the MBTI as a predictor of professional success. Others have defined it as "modern astrology".

Criticism aside, a paper by Naval Saini suggests that the strongest chess masters tend to fall into the INTP or INTJ personality types.[11] INTPs, known as the Logician personality type, love patterns and can foresee many moves ahead. INTJs, known as the Architect personality type, prefer structure and building solid positions.

In the corporate world, the ENTJ, ISTJ, and INTJ personality types appear to have the most billionaires. Thus, chess and business seem to share the INTJ personality type when it comes to achieving success.

Other models of personality

Within the analysis of personality types, the reduction of complexity to a manageable set of factors began with the "lexical hypothesis". This hypothesis posits that spoken language contains a reservoir of personality indicators, based on the principle that "if there is a word for a given trait, then this trait must exist". Guided by this principle, Allport and

Odbert identified 18,000 words in the English dictionary that describe personality. From this list, they extracted 4,500 words associated with permanent and observable traits.[12]

In 1946, Cattell organized the 4,500 adjectives into fewer than 200, which were later reduced to 35 by having various people classify their friends and acquaintances using these 200 adjectives. Subsequently, a factorial analysis was conducted to identify correlations between the various adjectives, reducing the number to 12. With the addition of 4 self-assessment factors, the total came to 16, known as Cattell's 16PF.[13]

The factorial analysis used by Cattell is a statistical method that reduces large sets of data to a few variables, or factors, from which the initial data can be reconstructed using appropriate linear combinations.

The Big-Five model of personality traits was also developed from Cattell's 16 elements through factorial reduction. The resulting five major factors are as follows:

- Extroversion, or the degree of activation, confidence, and enthusiasm in the actions we adopt.
- Pleasantness, or the amount and quality of positive interpersonal relationships that a person has.
- Assiduousness, or methodological accuracy and reliability, as well as the desire to succeed and persevere.
- Neuroticism, or the degree of resistance to emotional stress, such as anxiety, instability, or irritability.
- Openness to experience, or the disposition in seeking external stimuli to our ordinary context.

The personality traits of all the various models (16 PF, Big-Five, and MBTI) were put in relation to each other using statistical analysis to illustrate the correlations.

A particular correlation that clarifies the Myers-Briggs types is the one between Keirsey's temperaments and the MBTI indicators, summarized in Table 7.1.[14]

Decision-making processes and leadership

At the intersection of leadership and decision-making lies style, which can be defined as a set of attributes characterizing a leader's decision-making process. The phrase "It is not his or her style" is often heard when a leader makes an unexpected decision that deviates from their usual patterns in similar situations.

Leadership style is greatly influenced by personality but must be adapted to the circumstances. An autocratic style, for example, is inappropriate when the consensus of the group implementing the decision is needed.

Table 7.1 Correlation between Keirsey's temperaments and the MBTI indicators

ISTJ Inspector	**ISFJ** Protector	**INFJ** Counselor	**INTJ** Director
ITSP Professional	**ISFP** Composer	**IFNB** Healer	**INTP** Architect
ESTP Promoter	**ESFP** Performer	**ENFP** Champion	**ENTP** Inventor
ESTJ Supervisor	**ESFJ** Supplier	**ENFJ** Teacher	**ENTJ** Marshal

A useful checklist for determining the best leadership style based on the circumstances was developed by Vroom-Yetton-Jago,[15] a model for decision-making that's based on situational leadership. According to this model, the optimal leadership style depends on the following factors:

- Quality Requirement (QR): How important is the quality of the decision?
- Commitment Requirement (CR): How important is team members' commitment to the decision?
- Leader's Information (LI): Does the leader have sufficient information to make a high-quality decision on his own?
- Problem Structure (ST): Is the problem well structured (e.g. defined, clear, organized, lend itself to solution, time limited)?

Vroom-Yetton-Yago identifies three different leadership styles, each corresponding to a specific implementation process, summarized in Table 7.2. To determine the most suitable style and process for each situation, we can refer to the decision tree in Fig. 7.2. It relates the input factors (QR, CR, LI, ST, CP, GC, CO, SI), shown in the small white rectangles, to the optimal leadership style (AII, GII, CII, CI, AI), displayed as the output on the right:

In summary, a consultative or collaborative approach is more appropriate when:

- You need information from others to solve a problem
- The problem definition is not clear
- Team acceptance of the decision is important
- There is sufficient time to manage a group decision

An authoritarian style, on the other hand, is more effective when:

- There is a recognized authority
- The leader is confident in acting alone
- The team will accept the decision without objections
- Time is limited

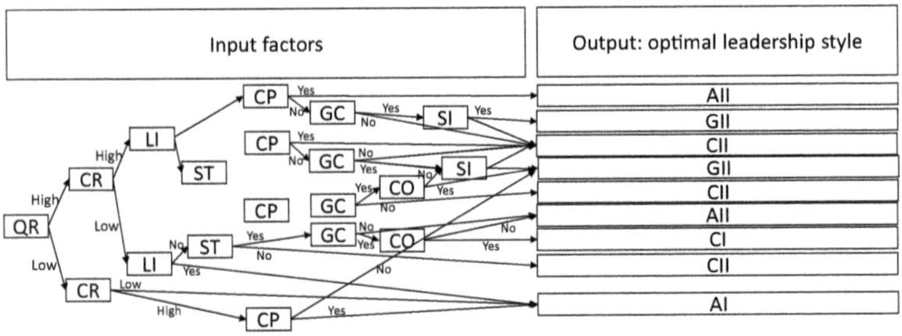

Figure 7.2 Optimal leadership style as a function of input factors

Table 7.2 Vroom-Yetton-Yago's leadership styles

Style	*Description*	*Process*
Authoritarian	The leader makes the decision and informs the others	Authoritarian 1 (AI): the leader uses the information already available and makes the decision Authoritarian 2 (AII): the leader requests specific information from others and, once collected, makes the decision not necessarily providing explanations on the use of the information requested
Consultative	Collects the information from the team and makes the decision	Consultative 1 (CI): informs the team about the context and information requested but the team is not involved in the decision Consultative 2 (CII): you are responsible for the decision, but gather the team to discuss the situation, listen to different perspectives, and solicit suggestions
Collaborative	Works together with the team to reach a consensus	(GII) The team makes the decision by common agreement, the leader is essentially the consensus-building facilitator.

The chess and corporate strategy leadership model

The chess and corporate strategy leadership model fundamentally hinges on the concept of intelligence.

In this paragraph, we will demonstrate how several concepts presented in this book directly connect to some of the most influential intelligence-based leadership frameworks.

First, De Groot's strategic thinking process has underscored two primary drivers within the decision-making process: the faculty of conceptualization or abstraction and the champion's arsenal or experience.

These two drivers are closely connected to the concepts of fluid and crystallized intelligence, respectively.

Raymond Cattell, the psychologist who introduced this distinction in 1963, described it as follows[16]:

- "Crystallized intelligence refers to the content of culture and educative experiences that a person has absorbed and can reproduce organized verbalized memories of them or habits associated with such content". According to Cattell, crystallized intelligence involves the use of learned knowledge making it directly related to our concept of champion's arsenal or experience.
- "Fluid intelligence refers to the ability to perceive relationships, to reason and solve problems of a novel or abstract kind that cannot be performed by relying exclusively on previously learned habits". According to Cattell, fluid intelligence involves abstract thinking, pattern recognition, and problem-solving, making it directly related to our faculty of conceptualization or abstraction.

Cattell's most notable finding is that fluid intelligence peaks around the age of 27, while crystallized intelligence continues to grow throughout a person's life.

Beyond experience and abstraction, other concepts in chess and corporate strategy reflect established corporate leadership principles. One such concept is the differentiation between strategy and tactics based on the speed of response to changes. This mirrors Daniel Kahneman's distinction between two modes of thought: "System 1", which is fast, instinctive, and emotional, and "System 2", which is slower, more deliberate, and logical. System 1 operates with rapid responses in situations such as driving on an empty road or making straightforward decisions in familiar circumstances, whereas System 2 engages in deep thinking for tasks like overtaking on a busy highway or making complex decisions in challenging scenarios.

Therefore, our ultimate message circles back to our initial point: intelligence is indispensable in the arsenal of a corporate executive, encompassing strategic decision-making, problem-solving, risk management, communication, and leadership.

In addition to intelligence, for a more pragmatic perspective on other leadership qualities that can be cultivated through chess, Samuel Hunt and Joseph Cangemi, in their 2014 article titled "Want to Improve Your Leadership Skills? Play Chess!", introduced a comparative table linking chess proficiency to corporate leadership skills (see Table 7.3).[17]

However, we can establish a more robust correlation between chess skills and corporate leadership by outlining the key skills we have explored in this book (see Table 7.4).

Table 7.3 Hunt and Cangemi's correlation between chess proficiency and corporate leadership skills

What chess is observed to be	*The true value of chess*
Capturing pieces	Control, interpretation, manipulation of real/perceived threats, gain/losses
Making moves on a game board	Planning/execution; maintaining equilibrium and building strong foundations for implementing relevant change
Manipulating pieces	Leadership, sacrifice, and knowing the strengths/weaknesses of key personnel for various situations
Defeating your opponent	Overcoming self-doubt, personal inadequacy, and becoming self-actualized through victory and defeat
Playing against someone else	Relationship building and collaboration; taking responsibility for one's own actions
Checkmate	Achieving mastery of the field/position, and turning potential victory into real victory

Table 7.4 Chess and corporate strategy's correlation between chess skills and corporate leadership

chess skill	*The value for corporate leadership*
Strategic thinking	Awareness of the mental process involved in making complex decisions
Decision-making	Mastering complex decision-making methodologies and avoiding cognitive biases
Strategic planning	Selecting the optimal strategy for each battlefield
Risk management	Managing risk and swiftly adapting the plan to new conditions
Negotiations	Improving the negotiation process

Chapter 7—Leadership—interviews

Luca Desiata interviewed by Bachar Kouatly

Can you provide a practical example of how playing chess has enhanced your leadership skills?

I distinctly remember how chess played a crucial role in enhancing my leadership skills during my transition from consulting to management roles. As a consultant, I was used to deeply analyzing corporate problems on behalf of clients. During this period, I played chess in long sessions, which matched the analytical nature of consulting. However, upon moving to management, I quickly realized that, unlike consultants, managers need to make rapid decisions. Initially, I felt uneasy making decisions without thorough analysis, fearing mistakes. Instead of learning through the trial and error of my own decisions, I turned to speed chess. This allowed me to practice fast decision-making in a risk-free environment where the worst consequence was losing a few games. Once I became comfortable with quick decision-making in chess, I applied this skill in my corporate role. Thus, chess helped me develop the ability to swiftly make decisions, facilitating my transition from a deep-analysis consulting role to a fast-paced management position.

Can you provide an example of how chess has enhanced your image as a leader?

During my MBA at INSEAD, when the new cohort arrived, we set up stands in the campus entrance hall to showcase the available leisure activities. I represented the chess club and, to attract attention, I challenged anyone from the new cohort to a chess game where I would play blindfolded. An Italian student accepted the challenge but played poorly, making two blunders in a row and resigning around the 15th move. Hundreds of people watched the game, and although many thought it was staged, it significantly boosted my reputation as a clever individual. While all chess players can play blindfolded to some extent, typically with a strength reduction of about 200 ELO points, therefore this type of play, though highly spectacular, shouldn't be seen as a surprising feat. Wittgenstein likened chess to a language, with a game being a form of dialogue. Thus, playing chess blindfolded should be no more surprising than seeing someone converse blindfolded. Here is how the Austrian-born philosopher would explain the parallel between language and chess: To understand the meaning of a word, or a sentence, you must already understand what you might do with it. A word or a sentence can be used to do something in the game that is our language. When I say "hammer", I expect that you will hand me the hammer (And you need not have had it explained to you what a hammer is for in order to know what to do with it after you have watched someone else use a hammer...). It is exactly in such a way that I expect that when I say "This is the king", you will understand that it has a certain role in the chess game.

The downside of my impressive blindfolded chess performance at INSEAD became apparent years later. Whenever my MBA friends invited me over for dinner, they would request that I play blindfolded against their children. While it was highly entertaining for the family, it demanded immense concentration from me, sometimes to the point where it affected my digestion due to the mental effort involved.

How long did it take you to become a CEO?

Excluding my role as Country Manager for France & Belgium on behalf of the Italian multinational electricity producer, which was an internal CEO position within the Group, it took me about 21 years to become the CEO of Sogin in July 2016, having started my career in December 1995. While I may not be a sprinter CEO, I certainly progressed faster than the average of 24 years, as assessed by the CEO Genome Project.

I had a strong CV with top grades from university, an MBA from INSEAD, and a track record of good performance in various international positions. However, what truly propelled me to be appointed CEO of Sogin was my unique experience in the nuclear sector—particularly notable in Italy, where no nuclear plants operate anymore. In 2009, after serving as Chief of Cabinet to the CEO of the Italian multinational electricity producer, I made the bold and risky decision to join Italy's nascent nuclear program. This move was particularly precarious because the project was canceled just a few years later due to the Fukushima disaster in 2011. While this choice initially made it difficult to reposition myself within the Italian multinational electricity producer, it ultimately paid off by providing me with a distinctive experience that was pivotal in my appointment as CEO in 2016. Although I wouldn't necessarily recommend such risky moves to others, I must admit that doing something unique can definitely make your CV stand out from the crowd.

In a company, what sets the absolute top performer apart from those in the top 100?

My appointment as CEO of Sogin was rather unique due to the specialized nature of the industry. Sogin is tasked with decommissioning old Italian nuclear plants and managing radioactive waste. My rare experience in the nuclear sector, in a country without active nuclear plants, was the primary reason for my appointment, beyond political affiliations or other considerations. However, when I found myself jobless after the Fukushima accident, I deeply regretted choosing the nuclear path over other opportunities following my role as Chief of Cabinet to the CEO of the Italian multinational electricity producer. Ultimately, the success of any strategy can only be judged in hindsight, much like a move in chess—its value is determined by whether it leads to a win or a loss.

How do you select your successor from a pool of candidates?

When I was the Country Manager for France & Belgium on behalf of the Italian multinational electricity producer, I was tasked with identifying my successor as part of the corporate succession planning strategy. I chose my CFO because he understood every aspect of the business in those countries and was well-respected by all employees. This decision was based on a combination of technical and leadership skills.

As CEO of Sogin, I initiated a talent program spanning all levels of seniority, from junior engineers to senior executives. With the Board of Directors' approval, I extended this program to include identifying a pool of suitable internal candidates for the CEO role. It struck us as odd that a technical company had never had an internal candidate proposed for CEO. Consequently, we identified a senior executive with a degree and PhD in nuclear engineering, an executive MBA, and extensive management experience over his ten-year tenure with the company. We discussed with him which additional roles would further enhance his understanding of the company, and subsequently promoted him to those positions.

Although the appointment of the CEO in a State-owned company is ultimately determined by the political majority at the end of each CEO's mandate, I was particularly pleased to see that the chosen candidate was the highly qualified internal candidate we had developed.

Anatoly Karpov interviewed by Bachar Kouatly

What makes the difference between being in the top ten from being number one in the global chess ranking?

My experience offers little insight into the difference, as I entered the world rankings directly in the top three. Everything happened so quickly that I couldn't pinpoint the factors and circumstances that propelled me to the top.

Today, chess theory and techniques have reached impressive levels, unimaginable to the champions of a century ago. This progress has left less room for inspiration and imagination. To excel in chess, one must continually work hard to refine their style. I consider myself fortunate to have been able to invest my best energies into an activity that suited my natural inclinations.

The main obstacle I faced may be hard for Western readers to understand, as it involved the bureaucracy of the old Soviet system. Each year in October, I had to submit a plan to the Sports Ministry for the following year's tournaments. Since major international tournaments, especially in the West, were often organized with only a few months' notice, this led to endless iterations with the Sports Ministry to update my plans. This process sometimes required even more time and energy than preparing for the tournaments themselves.

Unlike some of my colleagues, I felt comfortable within this system and maintained good relations with the ministry bureaucrats. Once I reached the top, these difficulties disappeared, and the Ministry became more accommodating. However, they were a significant obstacle to manage when competing below the master level.

I believe these challenges help build and strengthen character, leadership, and personal charisma, all of which are essential complements to technical skills. Chess is often viewed as a solitary and introspective game, but the dynamics of the world championship require exercising leadership over a team of highly qualified Grandmasters, each with strong personalities that can be difficult to manage.

In the past, the Grandmasters in the champion's entourage during world championships participated without pay, receiving only pocket expenses. Their primary compensation was the unique opportunity to learn. Therefore, the champion needed strong charisma not only to impose his vision during the analysis of positions but also to convince the Grandmasters to join him in a demanding and unpaid adventure.

The issue with today's champions is that while there are many skilled players, there is no standout leader or charismatic personality. This lack of a prominent figure might explain why the press, and consequently the general public, have lost interest in chess competitions.

What criteria would you use to select your successor from a group of equally talented individuals?

It's difficult to put into words, but exceptional talents are often recognizable at a glance. They possess a fiery drive, a deep enjoyment of immersing themselves in strategic complexity, and a genuine passion for the game's dynamics.

It is both a luxury and a prerequisite when we can align our true passion with our professional lives.

Which leadership qualities are innate and which are shaped by the environment?

Growing up in the Soviet Union during the 60s and 70s undoubtedly provided a highly stimulating environment for chess talent, particularly for a young boy like me from a remote Urals province. I began playing chess with the village's metallurgical team and won my first tournament against the tractor factory team. Had I been in a small town in America, I might never have become a world champion.

My family has always been quite neutral about my passion for chess. My parents have never attended one of my tournaments, and I never asked them to. The intense focus required during a tournament often makes a player irritable and leaves little time for relaxation. If my parents had come to support me, I might have ended up directing all that stress toward them.

Among the innate qualities, one of the most crucial is the ability to instantly "see and understand" a chess position. Study, exercise, and practice are meant to refine this vision and comprehension. With sufficient commitment and dedication, anyone can achieve the title of Grandmaster or International Master, as De Groot's analysis of strategic thinking suggests. However, moving from the top 100 to the number one spot requires this special gift of "seeing". Ljubojevic[18] used to say: you do not learn chess, you see it.

I don't want to give the impression that I'm downplaying the importance of determination and perseverance in favor of an innate gift that requires no effort. Tournament preparation demands a year of meticulous organization and discipline: waking up around 9 a.m., two hours of study, one hour of exercise, lunch, rest, two more hours of study, two hours of play, a walk, dinner, and games until midnight. This totals nine hours a day dedicated to study and practice. During the world championship, this routine becomes even more intense. To become a world champion, you must be prepared to sacrifice everything and live a monastic, secluded life, fully dedicated to the passion for chess.

For me, chess has always been both a pleasure and a natural inclination, so I never found the long training hours burdensome. As I mentioned earlier, I consider myself fortunate because my career aligns perfectly with my greatest passion.

What role did circumstances play in reaching the top? Can you identify one particular circumstance that, had it been different, might have hindered your path to success?

I recall one specific event that had a positive impact on my chess career. When I was 15, the Russian Committee made an error regarding my participation in a tournament in Czechoslovakia. The tournament was intended for adults over 18, but due to an inadvertent mistake by the committee, both another player and I, aged 15 and 17, respectively, were sent as Russian representatives.

I scored one of my best results ever. I won the tournament undefeated, with 11 points out of 13 (9 wins, 4 draws), beating the Czechoslovakian team for 3½ to 4 (3 wins, 1 draw). This outstanding performance garnered international attention and paved the way to more significant tournaments.

Another favorable circumstance during that tournament was that the three strongest Czech players—Kavalek, Jansa, and Hort—were absent due to other professional commitments.

Thus, two simultaneous factors contributed to the exceptional result that rapidly enhanced my international reputation: the error by the Russian Committee and the absence of the three top Czech players.

What is style?

Style isn't a shortcut for decision-making. Unlike strategy, which streamlines the process by grouping and quickly eliminating options, style relates to personal preferences and the enjoyment derived from playing one way over another. Since passion and pleasure are crucial drivers for reaching the top, style becomes a unique and essential characteristic of a champion.

A word of advice for those who want to follow your steps?

To dedicate and sacrifice your life to chess, you must be driven by a love for the challenge and for the beauty of the game. Without this motivation, the enormous investment of time and energy required to reach the top would be unjustifiable.

Follow your passions, whatever the profession of your life.

Notes

1 S. Hunt, J. Cangemi. Want to Improve Your Leadership skills? Play Chess! *Education*, Vol. 134 (2014), pp. 359–368.
2 "The Morals of Chess". Benjamin Franklin Papers. Vol. 29: March 1, 1779, through June 30, 1779. Yale University Press. p. 750.
3 L. Polgar. *Raise a Genius!* (Gordon Tisher, 2017).
4 https://www.tiktok.com/@chesszone/video/7168172452965649707.
5 E. L. Botelho & K. R. Powell. *The CEO Next Door: The 4 Behaviors That Transform Ordinary People into World-Class Leaders* (Crown Currency, 2018).
6 http://www.timothy-judge.com/Judge,%20Higgins,%20Thoresen,%20&%20Barrick%20PPsych.pdf.
7 T. Carlyle. "Lecture I: The Hero as Divinity. Odin. Paganism: Scandinavian Mythology." In *On Heroes, Hero-Worship, & the Heroic in History: Six Lectures* (London: James Fraser, 1841), pp. 1–2.
8 G. W. Allport, H. S. Odbert. *Trait-Names: A Psycho-lexical Study*. (Psychological Review Company, 1936).
9 H. E. P. Cattell & A. D. Mead. The Sixteen Personality Factor Questionnaire (16PF). In G. J. Boyle, G. Matthews, & D. H. Saklofske (Eds.), *The Sage Handbook of Personality Theory and Assessment: Vol. 2, Personality Measurement and Testing* (Los Angeles, CA: Sage, 2008), pp. 1–10.
10 I. B. Myers, & P. B. Myers. *Gifts Differing: Understanding Personality Type* (Mountain View, CA: Davies-Black Publishing, (1995) [1980]).
11 N. Saini. *Personality Traits of Grandmasters* (HalfChess, 2017).
12 G. W. Allport & H. S. Odbert. *Trait-Names: A Psycho-Lexical Study* (Albany, NY: Psychological Review Company, 1936).

13 H. E. P. Cattell & A. D. Mead. The Sixteen Personality Factor Questionnaire (16PF). In G. J. Boyle, G. Matthews, & D. H. Saklofske (Eds), *The Sage Handbook of Personality Theory and Assessment: Vol. 2, Personality Measurement and Testing* (Los Angeles, CA: Sage, 2008).
14 https://carrhure.com/blog/myers-briggs-types-versus-keirsey-temperament-sorter/#:~:text=It%20is%20based%20on%20the,and%20Idealist%2C%20Rational%20and%20Guardian.
15 V. H. Vroom & P. W. Yetton. *Leadership and Decision-Making* (Pittsburgh: University of Pittsburgh Press, 1973).
16 https://www.verywellmind.com/fluid-intelligence-vs-crystallized-intelligence-2795004.
17 S. Hunt & J. Cangemi. Want to Improve Your Leadership skills? Play Chess! *Education*, Vol. 134 (2014), pp. 359–368.
18 Ljubomir Ljubojevic, Serbian Grand Master.

Bibliography

G. W. Allport & H. S. Odbert (1936). *Trait-Names: A Psycho-lexical Study*. Albany, NY: Psychological Review Company.

E. L. Botelho & K. R. Powell (2018). *The CEO Next Door:The 4 Behaviors That Transform Ordinary People into World-Class Leaders*. Crown Currency.

T. Carlyle (1841). "Lecture I: The Hero as Divinity. Odin. Paganism: Scandinavian Mythology." In *On Heroes, Hero-Worship, & the Heroic in History: Six Lectures*. London: James Fraser, pp. 1–2.

H. E. P. Cattell & A. D. Mead (2008). The Sixteen Personality Factor Questionnaire (16PF). In G. J. Boyle, G. Matthews, & D. H. Saklofske (Eds.), *The Sage Handbook of Personality Theory and Assessment: Vol. 2, Personality Measurement and Testing*. Los Angeles, CA: Sage, 135–159.

W. G. Chase & H. A. Simon (January 1973). Perception in Chess. *Cognitive Psychology*,Vol. 4, no. 1, pp. 55–81.

K. Cherry, (2024). *What's the Average IQ?*. Verywell Mind. https://www.verywellmind.com/what-is-the-average-iq-2795284

ChessGames.com. Chess Database & Community. Accessed [2012]. https://www.chessgames.com/.

A. Damasio (1994). *Descartes' Error: Emotion, Reason, and the Human Brain*. New York: Grosset/Putnam.

R. Dawkins (1976). *The Selfish Gene*. Oxford: Oxford University Press.

A. De Groot. *Thought and Choice in Chess*. Amsterdam: Amsterdam University Press, 2008 (reprint)

S. Hunt & J. Cangemi (2014). Want to Improve Your Leadershlp Skills? Play Chess! *Education* Vol. 134, 359–368.

D. Kahneman & A. Tversky (1979) Prospect Theory: An Analysis of Decision Under Risk. *Econometrica,* 277–279.

J. C. Levinson (2007). *Guerrilla Marketing: Easy and Inexpensive Strategies for Making Big Profits from Your Small Business*. London: Piatkus.

B. Libet (1985). Unconscious Cerebral Initiative and the Role of Conscious Will in Voluntary Action. *Behavioral and Brain Sciences,* Vol. 8, no. 4, 529–566.

H. M. Markowitz (1952). Portfolio Selection. *The Journal of Finance,* Vol. 7, no. 1, 77–91.

H. P. Moravec (1988). *Mind Children: The Future of Robot and Human Intelligence*. Cambridge, MA: Harvard University Press.

I. B. Myers & P. B. Myers (1995) [1980]. *Gifts Differing: Understanding Personality Type*. Mountain View, CA: Davies-Black Publishing.

M. A. Nielsen (2015). *Neural Networks and Deep Learning*. Determination Press.

L. Polgar (2017). *Raise a Genius!* Gordon Tisher.

M. E. Porter (1979). How Competitive Forces Shape Strategy. *Harvard Business* Review, 57(2), pp. 137–145.

N. Saini (2017). *Personality Traits of Grandmasters*. HalfChess.

The Morals of Chess." Benjamin Franklin Papers. Vol. 29: March 1, 1779, through June 30, 1779. Yale University Press. p. 750.

A. Tversky & D. Kahneman (1974). Judgment under Uncertainty: Heuristics and Biases. *Science*, New Series, Vol. 185, pp. 1124–1131.

M. Vignesh. (Oct. 2020). Decision Making using Vroom-Yetton-Jago Model with a Practical Application. *International Journal for Research in Applied Science & Engineering Technology (IJRASET)*.

V. H. Vroom & P. W. Yetton (1973). *Leadership and Decision-Making*. Pittsburgh: University of Pittsburgh Press.

S. Zweig (November 4, 2021). *The Royal Game: A Chess Story*. Pushkin Press London, UK.

Index

For Product Safety Concerns and Information please contact our EU
representative GPSR@taylorandfrancis.com
Taylor & Francis Verlag GmbH, Kaufingerstraße 24, 80331 München, Germany

www.ingramcontent.com/pod-product-compliance
Ingram Content Group UK Ltd.
Pitfield, Milton Keynes, MK11 3LW, UK
UKHW021632240425
457818UK00018BA/375
9781032876443